Creating Extra-Ordinary Teachers

Also available from Network Continuum

Multiple Intelligences in Practice – Mike Fleetham

Pocket PAL: Multiple Intelligences – Mike Fleetham

Effective Teachers in Primary Schools (2nd edition) – Tony Swainston

Effective Teachers in Secondary Schools (2nd edition) – Tony Swainston

Learning Styles in Action – Barbara Prashnig

Pocket PAL: Learning Styles and Personalized Teaching – Barbara Prashnig

Power of Diversity (3rd edition) – Barbara Prashnig

Available from Continuum

Creative Teaching and Learning Toolkit – Brin Best and Will Thomas

Creative Teaching and Learning Resource Book – Brin Best and
  Will Thomas

Creating Extra-Ordinary Teachers

Multiple intelligences in the classroom and beyond

Branton Shearer and
Mike Fleetham

network
continuum

Continuum International Publishing Group
Network Continuum
The Tower Building   80 Maiden Lane, Suite 704
11 York Road   New York, NY 10038
SE1 7NX

www.networkcontinuum.co.uk
www.continuumbooks.com

British Library Cataloguing-in-Publication Data
A catalogue record for this book is available from the British Library.

ISBN: 9781855393905 (paperback)

Library of Congress Cataloguing-in-Publication Data
Shearer, Branton.
  Creating extra-ordinary teachers : multiple intelligences in the classroom and beyond / Branton Shearer and Mike Fleetham.
      p. cm.
  Includes bibliographical references and index.
  ISBN 978-1-85539-390-5
  1. Teacher effectiveness. 2. Educational leadership. 3. Multiple intelligences. I. Fleetham, Mike.
II. Title.

  LB1025.3.S528 2008
  371.102--dc22

                                                               2008021936

Typeset by Ben Cracknell
Printed and bound in Great Britain by Cromwell Press

Contents

Acknowledgements   vii
Praise for Creating Extra-Ordinary Teachers   ix
About extra-ordinary teachers   xi
How to use this book   xiii

1   Extra-ordinary teaching and leadership   1
Introduction   1
Writing the story of your learning and leadership life   4
What is extra-ordinary leadership?   6
Who will I become? Who will we become?   7
Creating your unique leadership path   12

2   The gift of multiple intelligences (MI)   15
A rough guide to MI   15
The MIDAS™ profile   24
Your personal leadership profile (PLP)   25
Create your MI leadership folder   30
MI in action 1: stress organization strategies (SOS)   32
MI in action 2: eight heads are better than one   35
MI in action 3: strategies to enhance your work   37
MI in action 4: inspired study strategies   38

3   Tools and techniques for extra-ordinary leadership   43
The five keys to leadership   43
Unlocking potential – something to RAVE about!   49
Leverage your achievement   54
The LEAD plan   55
Your perfect career   66
Careers associated with the multiple intelligences   69
Final GOALS   70

4   Being extra-ordinary in the UK and US   73
UK v US education   73
My long and winding road (or a student in the school of hard knocks)   82
US: six extra-ordinary journeys   88
UK: six extra-ordinary leaders   100

Conclusion   125
Resources and further reading   127

Acknowledgements

This book is dedicated to the development of your multiple intelligences potential. May you create wonderful paths to contribute to your community and to your personal growth. I want to express my appreciation to all my teachers and those many people who have sustained my work and to my wife, Andrea, who maintained her patience, optimism and enthusiasm in the face of the many challenges on the long and winding road. Special thanks to my father for his shining example and wisdom and to my mother, whose laughter lights up a room.
BS

To Fr. Martin Doe and John Warbrick.
MF

Thanks also to the following people for sharing their experiences:
Joe Burns, Unity College
Charlotte Gormley, The Compton School
Linda Marshall, Bradford Academy
Chris Neanon, Portsmouth University
Eric Pearson, Bradford Academy
Celia Walker, Solent Junior School
Lynne Williams, Glanffrwd Infant School, Wales

Praise for
Creating Extra-Ordinary Teachers

'Branton Shearer, a psychologist with expertise in assessment, and Mike Fleetham, a master teacher and teacher educator, have combined their respective areas of expertise in teaching, leadership and multiple intelligences. Their book is provocative, practical and disarmingly personal.'
Professor Howard Gardner, Harvard University, USA

'I commend this book to every teacher and educational leader who wants to inspire and motivate their students to better understand their capacity as learners. This is a very readable, accessible and fascinating book that provides the modern-day teacher with a practical framework to help them equip their students for their lives in the 21st century.'
Richard Chapman, Headteacher, Somerford Primary School and Archbishop Wake
     Primary School, UK

'The powerful message in Branton and Mike's work is that with a proper plan and a modicum of effort, teachers can indeed become extraordinary leaders in our classrooms. I'm pleased that this is not a prescriptive book, but instead is a guide for self-exploration centered around becoming *realistically* extraordinary. It is doable.'
Professor Scott Diener, University of Auckland, New Zealand

'This is a practical book that has simple strategies one can use immediately and is a valuable resource for all teachers. I will certainly recommend it to our Teaching and Learning Coaches for reflection and continuous professional development.'
Gillian Howarth, Teaching and Learning Consultant for Slough Excellence Cluster, UK

'This book is not only a must-read for people who are involved in education and teaching, but for any aspiring managers, CFOs and CEOs. I thought I understood multiple intelligences in its theory, but never was confronted with such a realistic approach to putting it into practice and hence improving my own personal capabilities.'
Count Andreas Graf von Faber-Castell, Managing Director, Asia Pacific A. W. Faber-
     Castell, Australia

'It reaffirms why most of us remain as ordinary teachers unless we ignite the spark within us that will propel us to develop and achieve excellence to become extraordinary teachers. Although examples are drawn from the Western settings, I found the approach to be easily adapted and applied to the Malaysian settings.'
Suan Yoong, Sultan Idris University of Education, Malaysia

'From the first page I was excited by the focus on MI in relation to extraordinary leadership. I can relate to all the wonderful ideas on leadership and being extraordinary, shared throughout the text. . . . Thanks for writing this wonderful MI source. I can't wait to include it in my list of references for all my students in future!'
Dr Pieter H du Toit, University of Pretoria, South Africa

'*Creating Extraordinary Teacher* . . . raises very important and significant issues tapping on everyone, not just teachers but people from every profession who want to make a change in this world.'
   Mania Ziridis, Owner of New Generation Ziridis Schools, Greece

'This book is inspirational as, for the first time, it sets leadership into the context of multiple intelligences . . . I would recommend this book to all teachers, middle leaders and especially to senior leaders as it will ensure all of us and our children fulfill our unique potentials.'
   Jon Le Fevre, Headteacher, Netley Abbey Infant School, UK

'An optimistic and refreshing book for enhancing intellectual developments for all our children and future citizens.'
   Professor Raúl Pizarro Sánchez, Universidad de Playa ancha de Ciencias de la
      Educacion, Chile

'The workbook is an easy read . . . and the stories invite you to ponder upon your own profile and make choices that may lead to entirely different life plans . . . Thank you for the privilege of allowing me to rediscover myself.'
   Gisela Lammerts van Bueren, Professional Development Unit, Panama Canal Authority,
      Panama

'Each one of us, as teachers, has the capacity to be an extra-ordinary teacher. This book explores ways to release that potential. It is fascinating, inspirational, accessible and 'in touch' all at the same time. Branton and Mike have expertly combined theoretical gems and extracts of exceptional practice with practical ways to move yourself forward . . . together this will make a real positive difference at 'ground level' in the world of education.'
   Lynne Williams, Senior Teacher and Teacher Trainer, Glanffrwd Infant School, Wales

'I loved the practical and reflective nature of the book. The message which came over strongly to me was that we have to look to ourselves, know ourselves, and then value what we do. We then appreciate how we can enhance this by being more of what we already are rather than recreating ourselves into some sort of new vision.'
   Chris Neanon, Principal Lecturer, University of Portsmouth, UK

About extra-ordinary teachers

Extra-ordinary teachers are leaders; extra-ordinary teachers inspire others; extra-ordinary teachers actively enrich what they do and help others to do the same. An extra-ordinary teacher celebrates when her pupils achieve. An extra-ordinary teacher is proud when his students' knowledge surpasses his own. An extra-ordinary teacher smiles when her learners independently make it in life, using the skills and qualities that she has instilled in them. Extra-ordinary teachers are in the business of creating confident, successful and well-rounded citizens of the twenty-first century.

Ordinary teachers spend their days plodding through the mechanics of teaching. They live from one pay cheque to the next. Teaching is a job rather than a vocation and the countdown to the closest holiday is paramount. Ordinary teachers are passive; they see no reason to change or grow and they feel powerless to go beyond simply delivering the curriculum. Their own self-imposed restrictions become the limitations of their pupils.

Any teacher can be extra-ordinary. Any teacher can be ordinary. Any teacher can be a leader; any teacher can be a follower. Most, if they think back, will have been all of these during their career – and for a variety of reasons: circumstances can be destructive or nurturing; opportunities can be relevant or meaningless. Sometimes we have control over our professional and personal situations; sometimes we don't.

This book is about taking (or taking back) control of your own teaching journey and discovering (or rediscovering!) the joy of helping others to learn and grow. It's about discovering the leader within you and enriching those skills and qualities. It's for anybody who is charge of any type of learning, in any organization, and who wants to get better at what they do. It's based on nearly 20 years of research by American educator Dr Branton Shearer and its interpretation in the UK by Mike Fleetham. Both authors are advocates of Professor Howard Gardner's theory of multiple intelligences (MI) and use it in their day-to-day work. Although the tools and techniques presented here are inspired by MI, they are not restricted to it. You don't have to be a champion of MI to take value from these pages.

How to use this book

Creating Extra-Ordinary Teachers can be used as a source book and as a workbook. It's a source of practical and effective techniques for enriching your own teaching and leadership, plus a workbook for putting those ideas into practice. We've divided it into four sections and designed it so that you can dip into the parts that are most relevant to your needs. Activities and quotations are scattered throughout, helping you bring the ideas to life immediately. This isn't a cover-to-cover read, but feel free to do that if you like!

Section 1 explains in more detail our concept of an extra-ordinary teacher and the notion of extra-ordinary leadership. Don't think you have to be in charge of a school or department to lead. Leadership is as much about innovating, taking a risk in your lessons and trying something new than it is about managing staff and explaining a vision. It's about being the one who steps forward.

Section 2 describes the theory and practical applications of multiple intelligences theory. It goes on to show four ways in which this powerful concept can be used immediately to enrich your teaching and leadership.

Skip the introduction if you are already familiar with MI, but do linger at the rest. Here we will introduce your personal leadership folder and Branton's MIDAS™ (Multiple Intelligences Developmental Assessment Scale) profile as a cornerstone to your self-development. There's a free online profile included with the purchase of this book. We recommend that you complete the profile and then have it to hand as you work through this section. Unlike other profiles, MIDAS™ delves deeper into each intelligence and provides the most thorough MI description available in the world today. MIDAS™ is also unique because it is a *starting point* for portraying MI characteristics and *not* a final, limiting end point. In fact, the first activity after receiving your MIDAS™ profile is to ask yourself, 'Is this correct? Is this really me?' And if you don't agree, you amend the profile!

To receive instructions for accessing your free online MIDAS™ profile, please email Mike Fleetham: mike@thinkingclassroom.co.uk with your name and the organization for which you work. Details will be emailed back to you as a .pdf (Adobe Acrobat) attachment. Please ensure that the return email address will accept .pdf attachments and mailings from the address above.

Section 3 extends the thinking of Section 2, with tools and techniques for becoming extra-ordinary. These include the five keys of leadership, the RAVE tool and how to create your very own LEAD plan. The focus here is on career development through leadership – both yours and that of your learners.

Section 4 provides two very clear descriptions of the UK and US education systems. We then offer you a host of examples that demonstrate what extra-ordinary teaching and leading can be, both in the UK and USA. These two countries are often ranked close to each other in international educational league tables and their school systems have similar strengths and weaknesses. A UK case study is culturally close enough to have meaning and value for a US educator. A US case study will make sense to a UK teacher, but we've described each system to clear up any misconceptions and to set the context.

The UK people featured are currently living, working and learning in the UK. The US stories are composite figures that illustrate how we each can take our 'ordinariness' and find that something 'extra' that can be leveraged to our advantage. We have chosen to tell the stories of these people because they exemplify the concepts of the extra-ordinary teacher and the extra-ordinary leader.

We finish up with a conclusion and a short list of further resources. We've gone for quality not quantity.

We believe that any teacher can be extra-ordinary and that all teachers can lead, either by example or by directing others. We hope that you will be inspired by the words and activities that follow to develop yourself and to show others the way.

1 Extra-ordinary teaching and leadership

Use Section 1 if you would like to:
- gain a more detailed introduction to the book
- reflect on your own teaching and leadership career so far.

Introduction

This book is a guide to the creation of a personalized path to the development of your extra-ordinary leadership potential. By the end of it you will know practical strategies for maximizing your own leadership abilities and the abilities of other people. The more that you engage with the ideas and activities described here, the more that you (and other people) will benefit from them.

You may follow the path outlined in this book for yourself, students, your children or perhaps people who you supervise. As a leader you wear many different hats. The mayor leads the city. Parents are the leaders of the family. Senior managers are mentors and leaders in the school. Children lead others in the classroom. And you are leading yourself on the path of your own development.

'Nothing great was ever achieved without enthusiasm.'

Ralph Waldo Emerson

Highly effective leadership is all about power and its management. We will explore what kind(s) of power you have to influence people. If knowledge is power then schools are on the mission of launching leaders who will have 'know how' and know what to do so our communities and nations will thrive. Educators will find the activities and perspectives of this extra-ordinary path appropriate for their work as leaders in the classroom and in their schools. Managers will find creative ideas here to further their roles as team leaders, visionaries and mentors. You can use this book to guide students to take full advantage of the opportunities available at their schools that will enhance their unique leadership abilities. Parents can also use these ideas to better recognize and appreciate how to encourage their children's full intellectual development and contributions to the life of their communities as adults.

As you embark on this path to extra-ordinary leadership you will do well to approach it like you would a grand journey through a foreign country. You could begin reading and simply do each activity as you read or alternatively you might first read it through as you would a travel guide or a map with several questions in mind, such as: 'How does this relate to my past leadership experiences?

'If one advances confidently in the direction of his dreams, and endeavors to live the life which he has imaged, he will meet with success unexpected in common hours.'

Henry David Thoreau

Can I use this information in my current situation to maximize my development? How might I apply this information to important decisions I will make in the future?' After you have read it through completely, you can then go back and do selected activities to meet your specific needs. Afterwards, gather your souvenirs and materials into your extra-ordinary leadership folder like a scrapbook. Finally, share your folder with someone who knows you well and discuss with him/her your reflections on what you have created. Snapshots from a journey are most appreciated when we share the stories behind them with a loved one. The joy and the meaning of the journey become clearer with each retelling. Hopefully, most of your initial questions will have been addressed during your activities and you can share your insights and future plans with your friend. At the end of this discussion, your immediate leadership objectives should be clear to you, along with specific long-term goals for your future leadership development.

You can follow this same process if you are reading this book to understand how to guide young people on the path to developing their leadership abilities. Many times people simply need an attentive and interested audience with which to share their thoughts, dreams and plans. Talking through our plans and then reflecting back on our experiences can be a powerful means of gaining insight and understanding. Schools can send the message to students that they are ALL expected to become engaged citizens who may take on leadership roles in an area of strength and interest.

If your goal is to advance into leadership roles at work then it would be good to first do an informal survey of people who are already in those positions to which you aspire. Ask yourself (and them, if possible): 'What does it take to do this job well? What are the challenges to managing? What skills are needed by educational leaders? What are the tasks and passions of classroom leaders?' Looking carefully at what these people do will help you to set your goals and plan ahead for your leadership path of development.

'I know the price of success: dedication, hard work and an unremitting devotion to the things you want to see happen.'

Frank Lloyd Wright

It has been said that people who fail to plan are planning to fail, but it is also said that every long journey begins with that single, first step. Achieving your goals may not be as simple as 1, 2, 3, but you will benefit from remembering to first: preview; second: engage; and third: reflect and discuss.

There are several activities to follow that you will want to complete to get the most benefit from this book. Reflect on your multiple intelligences strengths and limitations. Create your leadership folder. Consider the 'something to RAVE about' checklist. Complete the LEAD and GOALS plans. Do some creative thinking about how best to combine your multiple intelligences strengths into the 'perfect career'. You can also get some tips for managing stress, building self-confidence and strength-based study strategies. Lastly, write about your leadership life from the 'looking back perspective'. Is this too much? Only you will know for sure, but by offering a variety we hope you'll find an activity that suits your style and needs.

'Put your heart, mind, intellect and soul even to your smallest acts. This is the secret of success.'

Swami Sivananda

You may also pick and choose from these activities to best address your specific leadership questions or go through each activity one by one and see what emerges for you along the way. Do you want answers to specific questions or are you at a point where you will most benefit from creative exploration and discovery? As with many leadership questions, this is a judgement call that you'll answer as you act and reflect.

Can you find someone to share your leadership folder with? A formal or informal mentor perhaps? Offer to share this book with them in exchange for discussing your folder with you! You just might be surprised what you learn from this outside perspective. We often hear from even very accomplished people that they have gained valuable insights and self-understanding from this exploratory process – a variety on the UK practice of 360° feedback.

Writing the story of your learning and leadership life

Section 4 presents the leadership stories of many talented individuals. You may wish to turn there now to get an idea of the variety of ways in which people learn to lead. Or you might want to start at home, right where you are now, and focus on yourself. In Section 2 we'll create a personal leadership folder that will begin to tell your own story.

Extra-ordinary leadership begins with self-leadership, but it doesn't stop there. Developing your leadership abilities requires active involvement in a particular field and a community where your skills are valued. This can take place in your home, your school, workplace or in your community. We find it helpful to use the idea of servant leadership as described by Robert Greenleaf. This is a guide for directing your leadership activities to where they will be useful to others as well as to your own development. Greenleaf (1970), in *Servant as Leader,* describes servant leadership as:

'Make yourself necessary to somebody.'

Ralph Waldo Emerson

The servant-leader is servant first… It begins with the natural feeling that one wants to serve, to serve first. Then conscious choice brings one to aspire to lead. He or she is sharply different from the person who is leader first, perhaps because of the need to assuage an unusual power drive or to acquire material possessions. For such it will be a later choice to serve – after leadership is established. The leader-first and the servant-first are two extreme types. Between them there are shadings and blends that are part of the infinite variety of human nature.

The difference manifests itself in the care taken by the servant-first to make sure that other people's highest priority needs are being served. The best test, and difficult to administer, is: do those served grow as persons; do they, while being served, become healthier, wiser, freer, more autonomous, more likely themselves to become servants? And, what is the effect on the least privileged in society; will they benefit, or, at least, will they not be further deprived?

Activity

Storytelling: looking back

What will be the 'story' of your leadership life? Imagine yourself when you are retired and sharing the highlights of your life with your children, grandchildren or best friend. What would you like to include in this story?

You might consider, for example,

- What will have been the crucial learning experiences and perhaps accomplishments?
- How did you enhance the development of one of your key leadership abilities?
- Did you write that book? Did you become a persuasive speaker?
- Did you hone your sensitivity to the feelings of others?
- Did you develop effective personnel management strategies?
- Did you inspire others to learn and grow?

Tell your story in detail and dream how it might be told sometime in the distant future as you are looking back on a long and rewarding leadership life.

You might like to use your story to guide your personal leadership development. What would you need to do to make these envisioned successes a step closer?

What is extra-ordinary leadership?

We propose that extra-ordinary teachers are extra-ordinary leaders – whether they realize it or not. By definition, leaders are people that other people will follow. Howard Gardner describes two main types of leaders in the world. Direct leaders are in a position of responsibility or authority whose role it is to influence the behaviour of people directly. This is the kind of person that we usually think of whenever we hear the word 'leader' and obvious examples are our presidents and prime ministers, legislators, politicians, city councillors and the chairpersons of corporations, clubs and other organizations.

Indirect leaders influence people through their work or example. They are not the ones standing at the podium giving speeches, conducting negotiations, resolving conflicts among people or setting public policy debates. People who set a strong example in their field that other people emulate are indirect leaders. Great indirect leaders include Thomas Edison, the Wright brothers, Bill Gates, Bob Dylan and Peter Gabriel. An accountant who sets a shining example for others with her integrity, thoroughness and attention to detail is a leader to those who know her and her work.

We all have leadership potential, even if we don't see it in ourselves. We have found many similarities between the abilities required to manage a home and family and those needed to manage a large organization or country. In fact, ex-prime minister Tony Blair once famously stated that being a father was more taxing than running a country!

What is the secret to success? How can we change our ordinariness to become extraordinariness? How can we maximize our potential? Howard Gardner writes in his brief book *Extra-ordinary Minds* (1997) that the path to achievement is to:

> Discover your difference – the asynchrony with which you have been blessed or cursed – and make the most of it. Make your asynchronies fruitful, blissful. Take stock of your experiences – both those that you cherish and those that make you quake – and try to frame them in the most positive ways. Positive here does not necessarily mean self-congratulatory; rather, it means that you will try to understand what has happened or what you have done in a way that is most likely to work in your favour in the future.

In another book entitled *Leading Minds* (1995), Gardner describes how several individuals changed the world via their ability to communicate a powerful story that followers could easily relate to their own lives. This is why we have included several of these stories later on and encourage you to begin to write your own. An effective leader has a unique and intimate relationship with his/her group. S/he must maintain close and regular communication flowing back and forth between him/herself and the group. It must be a two-way street so that the leader is both deeply involved in the group and yet is able to stand on the edge to communicate a broader perspective that will lead the group forward.

To accomplish this delicate balancing act requires a set of skills that take time, experience, effort and guidance to develop. This book will inspire you to appreciate your multiple intelligences strengths and then leverage them to maximize your success and contributions to then making the world a better place. As you start to tell and write your story, the ideas and suggestions can be applied to both yourself as well as significant people in your life. Guide and nurture the leadership potential of your children, your students and colleagues. Include them in your story.

> 'Flaming enthusiasm, backed up by horse sense and persistence, is the quality that most frequently makes for success.'
>
> Dale Carnegie

Who will I become? Who will we become?

Are leaders born or made? Are you born with the skills and personality to become a leader or is it the influences in your life that make you so? People who become effective leaders are born with certain characteristics that circumstances and life experiences nurture. Many people never think of themselves as potential leaders because they don't seem to have the typical, traditional characteristics associated with direct leaders: extroverted, energetic, likeable, popular, talkative, and so on. Thus, they may wrongly label themselves as 'merely followers' and neglect to develop their abilities. Being a good follower is honourable and important, but limiting your potential to grow and contribute is both unwise and wasteful. There are many people who might benefit from your own unique form of leadership – direct or indirect. Conversely, there are some people who have all the typical characteristics of outgoing and enthusiastic leaders, but who do not have well-thought-out ideas, ethics or a sensitive understanding of their followers' needs.

Effective followership

Branton's father used to always say to him, 'Be careful who you step on on the way up the ladder of success because you just might have to face them again on your way back down.' Highly effective leaders never seem to forget that they were followers first and always will be. Learning how to be a responsible and contributing 'team player' is a foundational skill for leaders of every sort.

A combat sergeant wouldn't ask a private to take on a mission that he wouldn't do himself. A wise parent follows the good advice of his parents and learns from the experiences of his grandparents. The rabbi knows and follows the teachings of the Torah. American presidents follow democratic principles, the rule of law and the constitution. British prime ministers model British values. Leaders at the highest levels are followers too – of powerful ideas, boards of directors, their mentors, social trends, historical events or social movements.

It takes careful effort to learn the skills of the serious follower and the role of an effective team player. The jobs of assistant principal, headteacher, vice-president, secretary to the chair are invaluable and not easily mastered. Then it takes a leap of faith (and self-confidence) to dare to step up into a position of greater responsibility and complexity. There is some comfort in performing specific tasks assigned and defined by the boss and great satisfaction to be had in teaching others the skills you have struggled to gain.

> 'Success based on anything but internal fulfillment is bound to be empty.'
>
> Dr Martha Friedman

Will you become a leader, either direct or indirect? In a phrase, it is all up to you! Are you willing to put effort into stepping outside the comfort zone of the follower role? Will you pay attention to your field and followers? Do you care enough about what you are doing to put forth the extra effort and invest time in the betterment of others? If you decide to accept these challenges then it will be up to you to develop your leadership abilities to their fullest and then to use them in ethical and responsible ways that benefit both your followers and your own well-being. Leaders must take care of themselves as well as others to maintain their progress on the long and winding path to success. But if you do, then the rewards are worth it. Yes, you'll probably be receiving a bigger salary at the end of the month, but more importantly, you'll have the satisfaction of matching your skills to what others need and the pleasure of helping others to grow.

But what does it mean to be successful? It is good to ask yourself this question as you contemplate your leadership potential. An honest answer can make a great deal of difference in your ultimate destination. What are the most important signs of success for you? It is different for everyone, but of course, some of the most obvious outward signs of success are: money, status, prestige, power, luxuries, and so on. Or is there more to it than that?

Which of the following are of most importance to you? If you rated each of them from 1–10, which would be your top two? What would be your average score on these success measures? If your average score is above a 5 then you should know that these external measures are of some importance to you. There are also less obvious signs of success: happiness, a sense of peace and contentment, a happy family, learning something new every day and making the world a better place. If you rate these from 1–10 measuring how often you think about and regard such 'soft' signs of success, what would be your average score? Which one do you rate the most highly?

Activity

Your signs of success

1. *External:* rate each from 0–10, where 0 = not important at all; 5 = moderately important; 10 = extremely important.

   ☐ Money
   ☐ Fame
   ☐ Prestige
   ☐ Influence/power
   ☐ Luxuries (big house, great car, fine furniture, and so on)
   ☐ _____ Other

   Total score ☐
   Divide your total score ☐ by 5 = average score ☐

2. *Internal:* rate each from 0–10, where 0 = not important at all; 5 = moderately important; 10 = extremely important.

   ☐ Happiness
   ☐ Peace of mind/contentment
   ☐ Happy family
   ☐ Learning everyday
   ☐ Contribute to your community, improve the world
   ☐ _____ Other

   Total score ☐
   Divide your total score ☐ by 5 = average score ☐

Describe for yourself two areas that seem to be of particular importance to you at this time. These may not be the same as a few years ago and may change in the future. Describe if and how you would like these areas to change.

However, perhaps of more importance than your ratings are the areas that you describe as your focal priorities. Areas that resonate with you deeply at this time will influence your daily choices and life decisions in ways that may not always be obvious to you at the time.

As you create your own unique leadership plan or guide others through the creation of their plans, you will do well to keep the two or three highest valued signs of success firmly in mind. Too many people fail to get on (or remain on) the path of leadership that is right just for them because they give too little consideration to their own 'personal success goals'. Young people may pursue a path to meet the goals of their parents. A recent graduate may fight his way up the ladder in the pursuit of authority or status all the while feeling depressed and unfulfilled. A woman may sacrifice her teaching ambitions and remain in the shadow of her husband or the children where her natural leadership abilities remain hidden, unappreciated, dormant and frustrated. There is not one 'right path' for everyone so it is an error to use someone else's measures of success as you formulate your leadership plan.

'All outward success, when it has value, is but the inevitable result of an inward success of full living, full play and enjoyment of one's faculties.'

Robert Henri

It is said that leaders 'open doors to the future'. Thomas Edison lit up the world with his bright idea! Martha Stewart convinced millions of people that good eating and home decorating were important and within everyone's reach. Frank Lloyd Wright showed the world a new vision for architectural design. Tiger Woods has convincingly proven that he is the world's greatest golfer. Steve Jobs designed a computer that revolutionized the young computer industry. Eleanor Roosevelt demonstrated that government could function compassionately for the welfare of all of its citizens and not only the rich and powerful. *What can you do to make the world a better place?* This profound question can spark a significant change in your life when answered after careful reflection.

'If you do not ask yourself what it is you know, you will go on listening to others and change will not come because you will not hear your own truth.'

Saint Bartholomew

Another powerful way to phrase this question is: *Where will I lead? Is my current position making the most of my leadership skills?* Do you find greater value leading in your personal life among family and friends or at work? Maybe you will invest your efforts in furthering your development in community leadership roles such as youth groups, church activities or clubs. You may or may not have to choose from among these various leadership paths. If you are lucky you will be able to achieve a satisfying balance among your work, personal and community lives.

Your unique leadership potential consists of a combination of your personality characteristics and your abilities. Highly effective leaders have 'five keys' for solving problems, creating valuable products and providing worthwhile services. You will learn more about these keys in Section 3: people smarts, self smarts, communication, solving important problems and inspiration.

Creating your unique leadership path

There are many theories about what specific personality characteristics are needed to be an effective leader, but it very much depends upon the type of leadership role that you are playing. Great leaders have exhibited a wide variety of personality characteristics. Some have been extroverted and energetic while others are quiet, reflective and calm. Some situations require great charisma, assertiveness and drive, but other circumstances will benefit from a leader who works skilfully behind the scenes motivating and empowering other people to do their jobs well. Leaders use a complex set of skills, attitudes and behaviours to achieve their goals.

'Give me a man who sings at his work.'

Thomas Carlyle

One characteristic of people who are effective leaders for both others and themselves is 'mindfulness'. Ellen Langer describes mindfulness as being fully present in any given moment so that you notice new things and make new distinctions that other people may overlook because they are either thinking about the future or stuck in the past. Mindfulness is a powerful leadership skill when you use it to pay close attention to other people. Bill Clinton is reported to possess a lot of charisma because when he speaks with you he does so with his full attention. He notices and appreciates things about you that other people overlook or take for granted. As Langer (2005) says:

Mindfulness is the essence of charisma; when people are there, we notice. When you don't take the world as given, but as full of possibilities, it becomes endlessly fascinating.

So, indeed, you can work on increasing the power of your leadership charisma by being fully present and mindful!

Throughout history leaders have been described using a long list of personality characteristics, abilities and behaviours. Several studies (Bennis and Nanus, 1985) of effective leaders found three interesting characteristics that you will do well to keep in mind. Highly effective leaders:

- are endlessly curious
- persistently accentuate the positive
- always learn important lessons from their failures.

Effective leaders rarely dwell on the negative, but instead focus attention on building on the good and positive. A positive focus does not mean ignoring problems or negative information. To do so would be a sure road to failure. Instead, highly effective leaders acknowledge difficulties, but then focus on how positives can either be maximized or used to overcome the negatives. A positive approach and focus serves to maintain a sense of hope and open up future possibilities, but again, this should not be a simplistic 'Pollyanna' perspective that pretends problems do not exist or are unimportant.

'Problems are the price of progress. Don't bring me anything but trouble.'

Charles F. Kettering

Extra-ordinary leaders look beyond the surface level and what is obvious by being carefully observant and persistently curious. They strive to deeply understand by asking questions such as, 'Tell me more' or 'Could you explain that to me in detail?' or 'Tell me again why we do it that way?' 'What would happen if we did it this way instead?' 'How did we get that result?' 'Do other people think differently about this situation?'

High-achieving leaders don't let obstacles, setbacks and errors stop their forward progress. This ability to learn from failures is more than finding the proverbial silver lining in a dark cloud. This is more akin to growing the lotus blossom in the middle of the swamp. It is hard work to dig deep to understand the lesson inherent in any negative situation. It is not a pleasant task to ask yourself what went wrong and how did I contribute to this setback? Not-so-successful leaders skim over the surface, give up, blame others or plunge ahead to the next project without a thought to the source of their most recent mistake, misstep or miscue. Learning from failures is a hallmark of the effective leader.

'Adversity introduces a man to himself.'

Anonymous

Effective leaders don't depend upon luck or other people for their success. Instead, they integrate their problem-solving skills with their capacity for self-examination in order to maximize their chances for success. To engage in regular and rigorous self-correction requires a willingness to be both humble and determined to pursue the truth. When these qualities are then combined with listening to others for honest feedback (interpersonal sensitivity for community needs) then the average leader will know how to lead wisely. You will learn about these different key leadership skills in the following section.

Successful leadership is grounded in *self-leadership*. Bringing out the best in others begins with bringing out the best in one's self. Maximizing the skilful use and development of your abilities should be your standard operating procedure. It is important to understand what those gifts and abilities are and what they might eventually contribute of value to your world. A realistic appraisal of one's skills and abilities – without exaggeration or minimization – is essential to long-term achievement. Failure to look within with a critical yet kindly constructive eye can lead to frustration and setbacks. Bill Clinton's tragic downfall as a president is a prime example of a person with tremendous gifts who was unable to be critically self-observant when it was most necessary.

'To find out what one is fitted to do, and to secure an opportunity to do it, is the key to happiness.'

John Dewey

Bennis and Nanus (1985) describe positive self-regard as an essential characteristic of highly effective leaders:

> We can sum up what we mean by positive self-regard. It consists of three major components: knowledge of one's strengths, the capacity to nurture and develop those strengths, and the ability to discern the fit between one's strengths and weaknesses and the organization's needs.

Bringing one's strengths to the workplace is key to maximizing achievement. A leader does this for him/herself as well as striving to bring out the best in others in everyday life.

We all have strengths and limitations. We've yet to meet a perfect person. Yes, we've met a few people who thought they were perfect or parents who report their child is a 'perfect angel'. But, the truth is that we all have some aspects of our intellectual profile that are not as well developed as other areas. This is what it is to be human. We are not able to use all of our thinking tools with equal skill and facility. There is no shame in this. Rather than being fearful of the criticism of others, we depend upon the frank feedback from significant people to fully recognize our unique profile of multiple intelligences.

'If only every man would make proper use of his strength and do his utmost, he need never regret his limited ability.'

Cicero

2 The gift of multiple intelligences (MI)

Use Section 2 if you would like to:

- gain an introduction to the theory of multiple intelligences
- consider MI in school, at home and at work
- discover and understand your own MIDAS™ profile
- apply your MIDAS™ profile to personal leadership development
- use MI and MIDAS™ to create a career plan
- develop problem-solving and stress management strategies
- enhance work and study strategies with MI.

A rough guide to MI

The human brain is the most complex organ known. A typical brain is comprised of at least 100 billion brain cells and each of these neurons possess thousands of connections to other neurons. A thought or a memory consists of an electrochemical pathway among an untold number of brain neurons. These pathways are like trails in the woods. The greater the use of a particular path, the deeper and more lasting its impression on a network of connections and the easier it is to transverse. Every experience in your life etches itself upon your brain, so it is not an overstatement to say that *your* brain is unique in the world. No two brains are configured and wired exactly alike, not even those of identical twins. It is a major mistake to believe that you can accurately describe your true intellectual potential with a single number such as an IQ score. The human brain has many more equally important skills in addition to logical thinking and verbal abilities that comprise your IQ score.

What is intelligence? What does it mean to be *clever*? Is it related to common sense? Is it the same as wisdom? Does it involve creative thinking? Or is intelligence merely the ability to score highly on academic, IQ-type tests? Intelligence is an abstract term like love or beauty – its meaning varies according to the situation, but we know that effective leaders act 'intelligently' using a unique set of abilities required by the task and circumstances.

In 1983 Howard Gardner wrote his definitive work, *Frames of Mind*, in which he redefined the concept of intelligence by introducing the notion of 'multiple intelligences'. He argued that a person's intelligence varies according to '*how* you are smart', not 'how smart *are* you'. Most of us know someone who is academically intelligent, but rather incompetent in daily life and conversely, someone with a limited education but who can display remarkable abilities in other walks of life. Some of the most effective and wisest people around have had lacklustre (or non-existent) academic careers.

If you were stranded with an Aborigine in the middle of an Australian desert without food or water, he would be the intelligent one. Invite him to an office in the city and he would be fazed – he would not be able to operate your computer, and you would be the intelligent one. Gardner's basic idea is that there is more to being smart than that which shows up on an IQ test. Gardner helps us deal with this dilemma by defining intelligence as 'the ability to solve a problem, or create a product that is valued within one or more cultures'.

Based on this definition he goes on to describe eight distinct yet related forms of intelligence that are possessed by all people, but in varying degrees. Table 1 describes each of the multiple intelligences active in daily life.

	Activities	Study Skills	Just for Fun	In School	Careers
Musical	singing, listening, playing instruments	rhyme, rhythm, song, lyrics, repetition	hum, sing, drum, rhyme, compose, strum, whistle	band, vocal, composing, choral, orchestra	choral director, musician, sound engineer, DJ, critic
Kinesthetic	sports, dance, handicrafts, jogging, acting, mime, dexterity	gestures, write large 3x, act it out, dramatize it, make models	wrestle, touch football, soccer, magic, juggle, dance	recreation, dance, leisure, fitness, physical ed.	actor, coach, assembler, labourer, dentist, choreographer
Linguistic	speaking, reading, writing, storytelling, poetry	note taking, checklist, outline, tape record, teach	word play, poetry, storytelling, lyrics, read aloud	journalism, education, sociology, literature	writer, editor, librarian, teacher, translator, sales
Logical/ Mathematical	calculating, investigation, problem solving, strategy, logic	question, categorize, explain, analyse, compare	chess, mysteries, challenges, puzzles, computers	engineering, accounting, medicine, computers, science	lawyer, chemist, analyst, bookkeeper, engineer
Spatial	map reading, artistic design, crafts, mechanical	watch, map it, cartoons, visualize, colourize, notes	doodling, photography, modelling, clothing design	architecture, engineering, aviation, graphic design	landscape design, artist, interior design, pilot
Interpersonal	empathy, leadership, manage relationships	study groups, teach it to someone, role-playing, discuss	team games, sports, chatting, helping, volunteering	ministry, public relations, management	teaching, nurse, counsellor, sales, politician
Intrapersonal	personal knowledge, opinions, judgement, self-direction, goal	test yourself, ask why important to me, what do I know now	reflection time, surveys, planning life goals, journals	creative writing, philosophy, psychology, leadership	minister, psychologist, writer, artist, pilot, engineer
Naturalist	understanding animals, working with plants, science	use your senses, observations, metaphors	train a pet, fish tanks, nature hikes, plant flowers	biology, ecology, horticulture, zoology	naturalist, forester, farmer, botanist, gardener

Table 1 Multiple intelligences in daily life

(*Source:* Shearer, 2000)

The eight intelligences identified by Gardner can be recognized as natural talents – which each of us has to a greater or lesser degree. However, they can all be sharpened and honed. Your musical ability can improve by taking singing lessons and your linguistic intelligence will benefit from your participation in a debate class or studying the dictionary like Malcom X did while he was in jail.

Each of the eight intelligences has their practical, academic and creative aspects. For example, you may have a flair for home decorating and handcrafts, even though you never excelled in formal art classes at school. Your musical ability may be invested in playing an instrument with an orchestra, but your vocal skills remain undeveloped. We all have our own unique profile of skills and preferences!

'Some people are born to lift heavy weights, some are born to juggle golden balls.'

Max Beerbohm

Influential leaders gain the respect and confidence of their colleagues and followers because they have mastered essential skills in their field. Educators demonstrate keen interpersonal skills with students, colleagues and parents. Young people experience confusion when their aspirations are misaligned with their profile of abilities. Career success requires the mastering of a set of intellectual strengths working in concert. Leaders match their strengths to the needs and requirements of a particular situation or position.

Different leadership tasks require different combinations of several intelligences working together for smooth and effective performance. How effective a leader you will become depends upon how well you employ your various multiple intelligences strengths and also how well you manage your limitations. For example, some leaders are better at motivating subordinates while others excel at data analysis and still others specialize at imagining innovative solutions to complex problems. Your success will depend upon your ability to develop your unique capacities and find the best place to put them to use.

The multiple intelligences in detail

A word is a powerful thing!
Linguistic and logical-mathematical intelligences are most often associated with academic accomplishment. The core features of linguistic intelligence include the ability to use words effectively for reading, writing and speaking. Practical linguistic skill is important for providing explanations, descriptions and expressiveness. Academic aspects of linguistic intelligence assessed by standard intelligence tests include vocabulary and

reading comprehension. Linguistic activities requiring creative thinking include storytelling, persuasive speech and creative writing. Gardner describes the poet as the epitome of linguistic ability because of his/her heightened appreciation for the meaning, expressiveness and nuances of language. Other career fields requiring skill in this area include teaching, supervision, journalism, sales and psychology.

It's only logical!
Logical-mathematical intelligence involves skill in calculations as well as logical reasoning and problem solving. People strong in the academic aspects of logical-mathematical intelligence are usually described as being 'smart' or 'clever' (for example, mathematicians, philosophers, logicians). Logical-mathematical intelligence in everyday life is required for multi-step, complex problem solving and mental maths. Most IQ tests assess a person's ability to reason and problem solve quickly, but do not examine the creative and reflective aspects of the logical-mathematical intelligence, such as the identification of novel problems or the generation of new and worthy questions. Accountants, bookkeepers, mechanics, computer technicians and electricians all must use the practical problem-solving aspects of logical thinking.

That rings a bell!
Musical intelligence includes sensitivity to pitch, rhythm and timbre and the emotional aspects of sound as pertaining to the functional areas of musical appreciation, singing and playing an instrument. A composer requires significant skill in many aspects of this intelligence – especially involving creative musical thinking. On the other hand, musical careers (for example, instrumentalist, vocalist) generally require more circumscribed abilities that emphasize technical skill rather than creative output. Appreciation for the impact of music on our moods, social interactions and behaviour draws on the practical aspects of one's musical intelligence.

Just do it!
The kinesthetic intelligence highlights the ability to use one's body in differentiated ways for both expressive (for example, dance, acting) and goal-directed activities (for example, athletics, working with one's hands). Well-developed kinesthetic ability for creative movement is required for success in professions such as choreography, acting and directing films or plays. Precision, control and agility are the hallmarks of surgeons, dentists and athletes such as karate masters, professional football players and gymnasts.

Imagine that!

Spatial intelligence includes the ability to perceive the visual world accurately and to perform transformations and modifications upon one's own initial perceptions via mental imagery. Functional aspects of spatial intelligence include artistic design, map reading and working with objects. Visual artists and interior designers exemplify creative spatial thinking, and a successful architect will need both creative abilities as well as technical expertise. A car mechanic or engineer, on the other hand, does not need creative and artistic abilities to find the practical solution to a malfunctioning engine.

Follow your nose!

A person strong in the naturalist intelligence displays empathy, recognition and understanding for living and natural things (for example, plants, animals, geology). Careers requiring strong naturalist skills include farmer, scientist and animal behaviourist. Skilled scientists use pattern recognition to identify an individual's species classification, create taxonomies and understand ecological systems. Empathic understanding is a related ability that allows people to care for and manage the behaviour of living entities. Leaders can use their naturalist intelligence to understand patterns of human behaviour and to meet the needs that will promote growth.

The unique contributions of the multiple intelligences model are the personal intelligences. The intrapersonal and interpersonal intelligences are presented as separate yet related functions of the human brain (especially the frontal lobes). They are described as two sides of the same coin, where intrapersonal emphasizes self-knowledge and interpersonal involves understanding other people.

I hear you!

Interpersonal intelligence plays a vital function in a person's sense of well-being. It promotes success in managing relationships with other people. Its two central skills, the ability to notice and make distinctions among other individuals and the ability to recognize the emotions, moods, perspectives and motivations of people, are known to be critical factors in successful employment. The ability to manage groups of people is required for managerial or leadership positions. Good teachers, counsellors, salespeople, parents and psychologists need to be adept at understanding a specific individual and then managing that relationship.

To thy own self be true!

Intrapersonal intelligence is also essential to the management of one's well-being. Vital functions of intrapersonal intelligence include accurate self-appraisal, goal setting, self-monitoring/correction, and emotional self-management. Metacognition (thinking about one's thinking) is important for learning academic skills such as reading and mathematics. Intrapersonal intelligence is not the same as self-esteem, but it may be a strong factor in promoting self-confidence, self-regard and effective stress management. Well-developed intrapersonal intelligence is essential to one's sense of satisfaction with life and success. Careers that require skills in intrapersonal self-management include pilots, police officers, writers, administrators and teachers.

The multiple intelligences in school

Gardner never initially intended for MI to be used in schools, but once educators got wind of his theory, they realized that it described and validated their own beliefs about learners – that everyone is good at something. But moreover, it gave them a practical concept with which to design and redesign educational experiences. Here are several stories that describe typical school scenarios through the lens of MI.

Intelligence	Exemplary story
Interpersonal and visual-spatial and intrapersonal	Tyler always sat at the back of the classroom doodling as his teachers' lectures droned on and on. Most teachers dismissed him as 'unmotivated' and merely of 'average' ability, and his grades reflected this lack of high expectations. One day during literature class while reading *Romeo and Juliet*, Ms Albright noticed that Tyler's drawings were unusually red and swirly. She noticed that as the play was being read aloud that Tyler's face went through a subtle shifting pattern of emotional reactions to the story. She wondered if this was new or if she had simply never noticed it before. Maybe Tyler was actually listening and understanding the lesson! For homework she gave each student a two-column version of the first section of Act II. The text was in the right column and the left column was blank. Students were instructed to write their understanding of the text in the blank column. After class she called Tyler aside and suggested that since he liked to draw so much that he draw 'his feelings' about the plot, along with a few words or phrases that stood out for him and that captured the essence of the plot. To her surprise, Tyler offered to make a 'flip book' describing the story's plot. After the final test, Tyler shocked even himself with the highest grade in the class exclaiming, 'Hey, I finally know how to study so I really understand!'

Kinesthetic	Coach Mooney was a man of few words, but he was legendary for teaching by example. He always did the exercises and activities along with the students. He was not one of those gym teachers who stood on the sidelines and shouted as the students went through their routines. He was sweating alongside them. Sarah, a star swimmer, was in danger of losing her academic eligibility because she was failing Coach Mooney's history class. When he learned that she was also in the drama club he had an idea that changed her life. He offered students extra credit if they devised a project that would teach the class about the writing of the American Constitution. He suggested to Sarah and her swimming/drama friends that they do a skit with dialogue that demonstrated the compromises among delegates' positions as the Constitution was being debated. The result was an impressive 5-minute performance that raised all of their grades. Sarah was so inspired that after graduation she majored in history at university.
Linguistic and logical-mathematical and musical	Headteacher Smythe wasn't sure it was a good idea to play a rock song at a school board meeting. He'd been to every local group before explaining the school's finances in careful detail, showing point by point why more money was required, but still he was defeated. Now the music and language arts teachers were suggesting that he use the rock song 'Money' as a lead into his delegations. He also wasn't sure that having the slogan 'One Mill More Means Much' would work, but he was willing to try anything at this point as the budget holders didn't seem to be getting the message that more money was needed to keep the school operating effectively.
Naturalist	Science teacher, Ms Grace, was trying to think of ways to bring chemistry to life for her bored students. One day she enlisted the help of the cooks in the cafeteria and the head site manager. The project teams in the science class placed various food items in a clear plastic box on a shelf in the cafeteria. In the basement of the school she arranged for the same food items to be placed in a hot area near the boiler room and in a cool area near an outside door. Everyone (including the cooks and site manager) recorded their predictions about what would happen to each food item in the various locations. What surprised Ms Grace was that the best score of all was obtained by an SEN student who struggled with reading the science text but who turned out to be the best predictor of all! Now everyone wanted this boy to be on their project team.

Self-understanding

Having a realistic and valid description of your unique profile of multiple intelligences strengths and limitations has been called the 'royal road to learning, achievement and personal development'. You will already have some general ideas and insight into your abilities, but your leadership path will be more clearly defined if you create a detailed and descriptive profile. There are several ways to do this. A thorough and valid method is to complete the Multiple Intelligences Developmental Assessment Scale (MIDAS™) and then use those results to complete the activities included in this book. If you are unable to take the MIDAS™ online questionnaire, then the simple self-check described below will suffice.

> 'Never desert your own line of talent, be what nature intended you for, and you will succeed.'
>
> Sydney Smith

> To receive instructions for accessing your free online MIDAS™ profile, please email Mike Fleetham: mike@thinkingclassroom.co.uk with your name and the organization for which you work. Details will be emailed back to you as a .pdf (Adobe Acrobat) attachment. Please ensure that the return email address will accept .pdf attachments and mailings from the address above.

MI self-check

Review the MI in daily life chart on page 17.

Simply read each of the descriptions and mark the areas that you think are your top two areas with a 1 and a 2. Then mark the two areas that you think are your least well developed with a 7 and an 8. Now number the remaining four areas from 3 to 6. This will give you a starting point for describing your overall MI profile.

Remember that it is important not to base any major decisions or choices on this quick self-check without validating it for yourself. The full MIDAS™ guides this process so you may create a rich and descriptive understanding of your intellectual and creative life. The MIDAS™ profile will help you to make important life decisions more confidently and create your own unique leadership development plan.

To gain a sense of your leadership skills make a note of how you ranked your linguistic, interpersonal, intrapersonal and logical-mathematical abilities. This information will be used to create your personal leadership profile.

The next part of this section takes you in detail through your MIDAS™ profile and its use in creating your MI leadership folder.

The MIDAS™ profile

The Multiple Intelligences Developmental Assessment Scale is a self- (or parent-) completed questionnaire that can be administered and interpreted by teachers, counsellors and psychologists. The MIDAS™ was initially created in 1987 as a structured interview to assess the multiple intelligences profiles of adolescents and adults undergoing cognitive rehabilitation. It was then transformed into a self-report for ease of administration and three additional age-specific versions were created: MIDAS™-KIDS 'My Young Child' (ages 4–8), 'All About Me' (ages 9–14) and Teen-MIDAS™ (ages 15–18).

The MIDAS™ for adults consists of 119 questions that enquire about developed skill, levels of participation and enthusiasm for a wide variety of activities that are naturally encountered as a part of daily life. Validity studies support the conclusion that the MIDAS™ profile provides a reasonable estimate of a person's 'intellectual disposition' that corresponds well with other indicators of skill and ability.

There are eight main scales for each of the multiple intelligences and 25 subscales that provide qualitative information within each of the main areas. For example, there are three subscales for the musical scale (instrumental, vocal and appreciation). There are also three intellectual-style scales – leadership, general logic and innovation – that describe general intellectual preferences.

Numerous studies have investigated the reliability and validity of the MIDAS™ and the results are summarized in detail in *The MIDAS Professional Manual* (Shearer, 2007). Additional recent research papers are posted at www.MIResearch.org including reliability, construct, concurrent and cross-cultural validity studies. The MIDAS™ has been translated into 12 different languages and is used by educators and researchers in at least 23 different countries. The MIDAS™ is used widely by teachers and schools to enhance instruction and by counsellors for career planning. Psychologists use the profile as part of a multi-factored evaluation to understand a person's unique learning characteristics.

Completing the MIDAS™ profile is only the start of your extra-ordinary leadership journey. Many profiles like this are seen as end points that describe fixed and limiting skills or personality traits. The MIDAS™ is different. It describes you through self-reflection and a bit of clever computer processing, but is only the first step in creating a dynamic and evolving MI leadership profile. It grows and changes as you do.

Your three-page MIDAS™ profile will be returned to you via email, accompanied by a short interpretative pack. You should follow the steps outlined in this pack to create and validate your brief learning summary (BLS). This verified summary of your MI abilities can be used like a 'map' for a variety of purposes, such as career planning, stress management and educational enhancement. Your top two scales and subscales can serve as the focus for your choices and decisions.

In order to gain an understanding of your leadership potential it is now necessary to clearly describe your specific leadership skills and abilities by creating a personal leadership profile.

Your personal leadership profile (PLP)

Follow the steps here to create your personal leadership profile. This is similar to the process of creating the brief learning summary, but the focus is on your abilities pertaining to leadership. The result will be a concise summary of your unique profile of leadership strengths and limitations. This information will be essential to have when making decisions and plans to maximize your abilities. If you do not complete the MIDAS™ profile online, then you will have to use the MI in daily life chart on page 17 as the source for your information on your specific skills and preferences.

Activity

Creating your personal leadership profile

The MIDAS profile can be used to gain an understanding of your skills/abilities and leadership style. This is not an absolute test of your leadership potential, but instead you can use it as a 'map' to guide your future development and choices. Your leadership skills may be improved if you have the desire and resources. Leadership begins with self-understanding so you can lead yourself in the development of skills that are needed to manage, supervise and guide other people.

This brief learning summary (BLS) provides guidance for the fields and career paths that are best suited to your multiple intelligences strengths. It leads quickly to the creation of your personal leadership profile. Just follow the steps below to gain an understanding of your leadership abilities, skills and style. Use page 3 of your MIDAS™ profile report to create your personal leadership profile, or highlight specific activities and skills that are your strongest on the MI in daily life chart on page 17, using the table below.

1. Main abilities:

    Highlight these four main scales on your MIDAS™ profile (or the table below):

    Interpersonal   Intrapersonal   Linguistic   Logical-mathematical

    List them from highest to lowest in the 'main abilities' column in the appropriate area:

    High = 100–60;   Moderate = 60–40;   Low =40–0.

2. Specific skills:

    Highlight the scores for the following nine subscales:

    Rhetorical   Persuasion   Working with People   Personal Knowledge   Effectiveness Expressive   Writing-Reading   Problem   solving   Sensitivity to People

    List them from highest to lowest in the 'specific skills' column in the appropriate area (either on your MIDAS™ profile or on the table below).

3. Style indicators:

    Describe a memorable leadership experience that you have had. For example, 'I was captain of the debate team'. Also, from the bottom of page 1 of your MIDAS™ profile report write in the highest of the intellectual-style scales (leadership, general logic, innovation). These indicate if you tend to be more inventive, practical or social in your leadership skills.

	MAIN ABILITIES	SPECIFIC SKILLS
HIGH		
MIDDLE		
LOW		
Style Indicators:		

Validate this summary by discussing it with people who know you well and also compare it to other sources of information such as jobs you have held and feedback you have received from other people.

Now review the areas of strength and limitation and consider activities that will provide the chance to build your leadership skills.

Creating Extra-Ordinary Teachers © Branton Shearer and Mike Fleetham (Continuum 2008)

Activity

Self-reflection on personal leadership profile (PLP):

This summary represents areas of strength and limitation as described by you. This is preliminary information to be confirmed by way of discussion and further information.

The areas on the summary that I think are too high or low are:

	High	OK	Low
Linguistic	☐	☐	☐
Intrapersonal	☐	☐	☐
Interpersonal	☐	☐	☐
Logical-mathematical	☐	☐	☐

Overall, I think the profile is: OK ☐   too high ☐   too low ☐   mixed up ☐

My _____ scale surprises me because:

_____

_____

My _____ scale puzzles me because:

_____

_____

What I learned about myself by completing this assessment is:

_____

Specific skills associated with my leadership strengths are: _____

_____

_____

_____

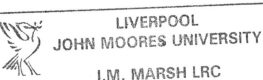

Reviewing leadership scales

The MIDAS™ assessment provides information to help you understand your abilities better so you may be successful in life and make a positive contribution to the world. Your brief learning summary will provide guidance about career pathways where your chances for success will be maximized. The personal leadership profile will guide you in understanding some of the basic skills necessary to develop your leadership effectiveness. All of these abilities may be improved over time and with effort and guidance. It is up to you decide how much time and effort you are willing to invest in developing them. Most people are content to be followers and competent team players, while others desire to assume positions of greater leadership responsibility.

Leadership can take many forms. Some people lead indirectly by example and set high standards for performance in a particular field. For example, a salesperson may set sales records through the innovative use of visual materials to augment presentations. Colleagues and others may emulate this approach to the degree where the whole field of marketing and sales may be changed by following this person's example.

There are also leaders who manage, supervise and guide other people in the community, on the job and even at home. Parents are the leaders of their children and grandparents traditionally provide guidance for the parents. Mayors and city counsellors create laws that guide the future of their community.

Effective leaders require many skills in their daily task of working with people and guiding them into a better future. There are three areas of leadership that the MIDAS™ assessment will profile for your benefit. The first task of the effective leader is self-management and self-understanding. The second task is to understand other people and how to manage them. The third fundamental skill for the leader is communication.

Intrapersonal:
- What are your strengths? What are your limitations?
- What field or career path is the best for you?
- Can you manage your professional, personal and emotional lives?
- Can you set realistic goals, plan and work methodically towards them?

Interpersonal:
- Can you easily understand the ideas and feelings of other people?
- Can you help people to work together to achieve a goal?

- Do you recognize the best in people?
- Can people trust you to have their best interests in mind?

Communication:

- What is your best means of communication?
- Are you good with spoken or written communication?
- Can you effectively share your ideas?
- Are people motivated by your example, ideas or words?

These main and subscales on your MIDAS™ relate to your leadership style and strengths. Review these definitions to determine how your personal leadership profile can guide your next steps in the development of your potential. If you do not have a MIDAS™ profile then you can highlight similar activities on the MI in daily life chart on page 17.

Leadership abilities

- Interpersonal: *To think about and understand another person. To have empathy and recognize distinctions among people and to appreciate their perspectives with sensitivity to their motives, moods and intentions. It involves interacting effectively with one or more people in familiar, casual or working circumstances.*

  Social sensitivity: sensitivity to/understanding of other people's moods, feelings and point of view.

  Social persuasion: ability for influencing other people.

  Interpersonal work: interest and skill for jobs involving working with people.

- Intrapersonal: *To think about and understand one's self. To be aware of one's strengths and weaknesses and to plan effectively to achieve personal goals. Reflecting on and monitoring one's thoughts and feelings and regulating them effectively. The ability to monitor one's self in interpersonal relationships and to act with personal efficacy.*

  Personal knowledge/efficacy: awareness of one's own ideas, abilities; to achieve personal goals.

  Calculations: metacognition 'thinking about thinking' involving numerical operations.

  Spatial problem solving: self-awareness to problem-solve moving self or objects through space.

  Effectiveness: ability to relate oneself well to others and manage personal relationships.

- Linguistic: *To think in words and to use language to express and understand complex meanings. Sensitivity to the meaning of words and the order among words, sounds, rhythms, inflections. To reflect on the use of language in everyday life.*

  Expressive sensitivity: skill in the use of words for expressive and practical purposes.

  Rhetorical skill: to use language effectively for interpersonal negotiation and persuasion.

  Written-academic: to use words well in writing reports, letters, stories, verbal memory, reading.

- Leadership: *To use language effectively to organize and solve interpersonal problems and goals.*

- General logic: *To deal with problems in an intuitive, rapid and perhaps unexpectedly accurate manner ... to bring together a wide amount of information and to make it part of a general and effective plan of action.*

- Innovation: *To work in artistic, divergent and imaginative ways. To improvise and create unique answers, arguments or solutions.*

Create your MI leadership folder

You are now ready to make you extra-ordinary MI leadership folder. This will stay with you during your leadership journey to record your starting points, your aims, your successes and challenges.

It is a visual representation of your multiple intelligences leadership strengths and limitations. You can use your MI leadership folder to store your MIDAS™ profile and other written materials.

Activity

Create your MI leadership folder

Purpose:

This activity will provide you with an opportunity to create a visual representation of your MI strengths and weaknesses. Cutting and pasting visual images onto the front and back of your folder will give you time to reflect on practical MI activities. You can use this folder to gather your MI materials while reading this book and have a special place where you know you will be able to find them as a resource in the future.

Materials:

- large folder, with pockets
- old magazines   • markers   • stickers
- assorted craft materials   • tape or glue stick

Procedure:

For this exercise you should focus on the MIDAS™ scales most associated with leadership: linguistic, interpersonal, intrapersonal and logical-mathematical.

Review your MIDAS™ personal leadership profile and make note of three to four specific skills in your two areas of leadership strength. Also, note particular areas of limitation in your two lowest leadership scales. You may want to reflect on the MI leading tips list provided in the materials that came with your online profile.

Try to find a few pictures in magazines (or create them) that represent actual leadership activities that pertain to you. Second, find (or make) images that represent leadership activities in your areas of limitation that rarely (or never) find their way into your life. You might also consider marking the front and back of your folder with song titles or lyrics that capture something distinctive about your MI leadership profile, for example, '*I Did It My Way*!'

Reflections:

Discuss your folder with a colleague or someone who knows you well. Ask for their opinion on your profile of strengths and limitations. Do they agree that it is accurate? Are there areas of weakness that might be important for you to improve in order to enhance your chances for success? Does your friend have any suggestions?

Consider subordinates, followers or team-mates of yours who have weaknesses in your areas of strength. Do they feel valued, neglected or unmotivated?

Do you feel comfortable with this form of visual communication? Any surprises? If it's not a strength for you, do you see its potential value? In what other ways could you assemble a record of your extra-ordinary leadership journey?

You are now ready to bring your enhanced self-knowledge to bear on real situations. In Section 3 we'll get to more of the strategic aspects of leadership. For now, here are several leadership tools for yourself and for those with whom you work and teach. Use them in order or pick the one that is most relevant to you.

MI in action 1: stress organization strategies (SOS)

Leadership can be stressful. With power comes responsibility; with innovation comes risk. Leaders recognize the need to manage stress effectively, to relax and to enable others to do the same. Consider your MI strengths. They are likely to be the most effective when you need to manage stress. Think about your weaknesses – they may hold hidden potential to relax you when your favoured methods lose their novelty or potency. Here are many MI-related ideas for you to try out. Record their effectiveness in your folder.

Intrapersonal strategies:
- keep a stress diary
- recall times in the past when you survived under stress
- recall positive affirmations
- remember to exercise your strengths
- reward yourself for taking steps to eliminate stressors
- identify negative feelings that you're holding inside
- remember to practice slow, deep breathing
- list your own personal priorities and values
- other _____.

Linguistic strategies:
- read a comforting, entertaining or soothing book
- listen to a humorous book on audiotape
- write a diary entry describing your pressure or stressors
- express your feelings via art, writing or talking it out
- ask others to tell their story about relaxing and managing stress
- go to the library
- read (write) poetry or song lyrics
- monitor and eliminate negative self-talk
- practise being your own enthusiastic cheerleader
- talk out your stress with a good friend, family member or counsellor

- other _____.

Spatial strategies:
- think of an image that makes you smile or laugh
- review your old photo albums and relive the good times
- assemble a puzzle
- work on a favourite craft project
- rearrange the furniture or redecorate a room
- fix or repair something that is broken
- create a card for someone you care about
- take a mini-holiday via your daydreaming
- watch a classic favourite film
- visit a museum or art gallery
- go to a craft shop or hardware shop
- clean and work on your car
- spend time in your workshop just pottering around
- other _____.

Kinesthetic strategies:
- go for a walk or a jog
- exercise or lift weights
- dance in your living room wildly
- invite friends to go out dancing on Friday night
- work on a woodworking project
- tackle a home improvement project that you've been wanting to do
- have a massage or exchange massages with a friend
- take up knitting, sewing, cross-stitch or crochet
- learn progressive muscle relaxation techniques
- tinker with things or build a model or refinish old furniture
- pay attention to slowing down your breathing
- give yourself movement breaks on especially stressful days (or everyday!)
- go golfing, fishing or roller skating
- exercise
- other _____.

Logical-mathematical strategies:
- measure the amount of stress in each day on a scale from 1–10
- categorize the different types of stress/pressures in your life
- explain in step-by-step detail how you will begin to manage stress
- analyse the type, source and degree of your stressors
- experiment with different types of stress reduction techniques

- play a relaxing strategy game
- get your life organized
- study the science of stress and its effects on the body
- play with riddles, puzzles or breaking codes
- other _____.

Interpersonal strategies:
- talk with a best friend, family member or counsellor
- offer to help someone to get your mind off your problems
- go to the theatre to watch a play
- take acting lessons
- join a new social club
- volunteer at the church
- take on a leadership position
- coach a children's team
- read aloud to children at the library
- visit someone you love or care about
- other _____.

Musical strategies:
- listen to music that relaxes you
- sing as loudly as you can
- beat on a drum until you are sweaty and tired
- get together with friends for singing
- create a song that matches your mood
- learn to play a new instrument
- make up a song lyric that amuses you
- teach someone else how to play your favourite instrument
- match your breathing to music that soothes and calms you
- other _____.

Naturalist strategies:
- observe something carefully and identify patterns in your daily stress
- record and organize data into a system that makes sense
- brush your dog or cat
- take the dog (or a friend's dog) for a nice long relaxing walk
- go to the zoo or aquarium
- volunteer at the local animal shelter
- discover how your stress has developed over time and look for growth
- imagine how you are cultivating new knowledge to feed your mind
- other _____.

MI in action 2: eight heads are better than one

As we will see in the next section, problem solving is a key element of extra-ordinary leadership. Leaders are often tasked with thinking up innovative solutions. MI provides multiple starting points for attacking and addressing difficulties:

Activity

Problem solving

Select a 'problem situation' or concern to be resolved – real or imagined. In a small group perform these actions:

- Linguistic: Write the idea or topic clearly in your own words as much as possible.
- Logical-mathematical: Speculate on the possible causes of this situation/problem. List four or five. Now rank them according to most probable or of most influence to least. Discuss how many people are affected or are involved. How many sub-types or groups or categories are involved. Create a pie chart to show the proportions and/or create an equation to show interaction among the elements of the situation. Is there a pattern? Can you imagine a timeline of events with cause and effect explanations between each event?
- Spatial: What image comes to mind when you describe this situation to yourself or to someone else? Is there a colour, design or symbol that would clearly represent some issue or feeling? Could you imagine or sketch a series of cartoon drawings that would demonstrate the different components or events in the situation? Imagine what you might do or say in the near future that would contribute to improving this problem. What would the problem look like in ten years?
- Musical: What song title, nursery rhyme or catchy slogan does this situation remind you of? What might be the refrain of a song about this situation? If you can't think of any old or recent songs then make up a refrain or chant.
- Kinesthetic: What gestures or sequence of movements/actions express something about this situation or its possible change or resolution? Are there any types of dance that embody it, for example the twist, the foxtrot, graceful ballet, or tightrope walking, walking on hot burning coals, and so on.
- Interpersonal: Describe the perspectives (agendas, priorities, values), feelings and motivations of the major players in the situation. Who assumes the leadership role and who the follower? Who is the real power behind the throne? Who has made efforts to improve the situation? Why couldn't s/he accomplish the task? Who might have the skills and resources to help? What do the people in power need from followers and vice versa?
- Intrapersonal: When you think of this situation what feelings do you have about your part in it? Frustration, glee, sadness, hopefulness, despair, anger . . . Why did you act in a particular way in regard to it? How might you act differently now? What personal strengths do you have that could be usefully employed? What would be your goal?
- Naturalist: How does this situation live within or impact on the natural world? Is there in the natural world a model for how you might solve this problem?

Read your original description of the problem. How might you rewrite it now? Do you see it or feel differently about it now? Can you imagine a more positive outcome that you didn't previously?

Creating Extra-Ordinary Teachers © Branton Shearer and Mike Fleetham (Continuum 2008)

MI in action 3: strategies to enhance your work

Each new MI leadership tool that you activate can provide you with more power to solve problems, provide services and create products that have value. The following are a few key strategies that you may keep in mind and refer to whenever you are in need of inspiration.

Intrapersonal:

- How do you feel about a situation?
- What do you already know?
- What are your goals and expectations?
- How can you best manage and decrease your stress?
- What do you need to do your job the best?
- Remember to monitor your progress and seek out feedback.
- How will you know if you have accomplished your objective?
- Engage in post-mortem review of your project.

Interpersonal:

- Acknowledge feelings of people.
- Consider other people's viewpoints.
- Describe their expectations, needs and desires.
- Identify the strengths and weaknesses of other people involved.
- Describe salient personality characteristics.
- What do people already know about the situation/topic, and so on?
- What negotiation strategies will help you deal with a situation?
- Describe the general mood of the group.

Linguistic:

- Communicate in clearly written prose.
- Use memorable phrases and define unfamiliar terms.
- What is the main theme or memorable story you have to tell?
- Use persuasive speech or point-counterpoint debate.
- Take careful notes or use a tape recorder to record important ideas.

Visual-spatial:

- Can you conjure a powerful image in the mind's eye of people?
- When teaching use demonstration, visualization and sketching.
- Use evocative metaphors, analogies or exaggerated images to communicate.
- Use pictures, videos, Power Point, posters or props to communicate.

Kinesthetic:

- Observe the message of listeners' 'body language'.
- Give listeners a stretch-break energizer (after 20+ minutes).
- Can you use or encourage participants to use gestures or body movements?
- When thinking through a problem role-play or physically enact it.
- Write your notes LARGE or over and over again.

Musical:

- Incorporate a piece of music while working.
- Instruct with a song lyric/rhyme/haiku that captures your point.
- Modulate your voice quality to engage listener.
- Encourage employees to incorporate music into their work.

Naturalist:

- Look for patterns in behaviour or recurring problems.
- Wonder aloud how the problem or task nurtures life.
- Is there an animal/plant metaphor appropriate to your project/topic?
- What are the ecological implications of your work?

Logical-mathematical:

- Explain a task or procedure step by step, in detail.
- Accentuate and highlight the logical progression of your ideas.
- Reveal cause and effect and relationships among ideas.
- Provide all pertinent statistics.
- Create a simple graph or chart to illustrate essential information.
- Collect data, compare and critique.
- Question, how, why and what.

MI in action 4: inspired study strategies

Whether you are studying for yourself or supporting your learners, different MI strengths suggest different approaches to the hard craft of learning material for recall. Here are several descriptions of how to study for those with differing intelligences strengths.

Linguistic

How to study:

I can use linguistic activities to learn anything! I will read everything in the book carefully. I will listen especially to explanations and write detailed notes, which I can then rewrite and translate into my own words. I will pick out keywords to memorize. I will build my vocabulary. I will learn the meaning of words that confuse me. I can use a tape recorder to help me study by talking out loud and then listening to the recording. I can make up a story. I can create a rhyme to help me remember. I can talk to someone about what I'm trying to learn and try to teach, convince or sell to them this new information. I will write a checklist of everything I need to know. I can make an outline of the information.

Spatial

How to study:

I can use my spatial, imagination and artistic abilities to learn anything! I can organize my notes on the page in a clear design. I can use 'mapping' to visually arrange new information. I can use different coloured pens, markers, paper or notebooks. I will visualize 'real-life' situations involving the information. I can do some drawing or building before reading to warm up my brain. I can picture myself knowing how to use the new information very well on a test or project. I will look to see how the whole problem works from beginning to end and then break it down into chunks and pieces. I can use doodles, drawings or other symbols to help me memorize things. I can make cartoons or a videotape to explain complicated ideas and practise skills. I can ask someone to show me how it works while I watch carefully.

Kinesthetic

How to study:

I can use my body to learn anything! I can try moving around while I study. I can take movement breaks or walk while I study my notes. I can manually write out the information over and over. I can 'do it' not just talk about it. I can get a feel for it and follow hunches. I can physically sort out my notes and rearrange the information using note cards. I will practise, practise and practise. I will try to imitate exactly how someone else does it. I can find ways to act out or dramatize the information. I can play make believe and pantomime it. I can invent gestures to describe what I'm learning. I can tinker with it and build a model.

Logical-mathematical

How to study:

I can use my logical skills to learn anything! I can use logic to find explanations for how things work. I can create detailed plans about connections and relationships between things. I can seek out solutions like a detective. I can make a game and challenge myself to find a more efficient and better way to study. I can test myself and analyse my mistakes. I can count my errors and chart my progress. I can tackle a problem in an orderly way: first things first. I can often ask WHY and HOW. I can outline the logical pattern of the information and determine what's most important and least. I will wonder about the possibilities and test out answers. I can draw a timeline of events with logical explanations of the connections between each event.

Interpersonal

How to study:

I can use my interpersonal skills to learn anything! I can try very hard to understand what the teacher wants me to be able to do and what to know. I will 'read his mind' and then check it out to see if I am right. I will ask two or three people in the class or a friend what I am supposed to know. I will ask the student who is a whiz to explain it to me. I will have fun 'playing the role' of the person who is an expert. I will lead a 'study group'. I will talk to a best friend on the phone and we'll study it together. I will do my best to teach the new information to someone else and then have them teach it back to me. I will be my own best cheerleader while I am learning something very difficult. I will remind myself that someone important is counting on me to do my best. I will try to sell or persuade someone that I am an expert. I will dramatize the information.

Intrapersonal

How to study:

I can use my intrapersonal skills to improve my learning in anything! I can first ask myself, 'What do I already know about this?' and 'Why is this information important to me? How do I feel about it now? How does it fit in my life and my future? Will I ever need to know or use this?' I can slow down my practice or study process to find and correct my mistakes or misunderstandings. I will review my work often and ask myself, 'What did I just learn? Is it important to know and remember?' As I study a new subject I will remind myself of what my learning strengths are and try to use them to learn. If I become discouraged or frustrated or sidetracked I will think of ways to focus my thoughts and think positive. I will learn to test myself to discover if I am learning. I will not put myself down because of my weaknesses. I will find ways to boost my self-confidence and not give up. I will use positive self-talk when solving problems. I will remind myself that I am my own best teacher. I will check out my new learning with teachers or parents to be sure I have studied correctly.

Musical

How to study:

I can use my musical skills to learn anything! I can play familiar or relaxing music before or during my study time. I can make up fun rhymes or lyrics using new information I must memorize. I will listen for rhythms and sound patterns in explanations. I can energize my brain to study when I'm tired with strong music. I can hum to myself as I do my work. I can take musical breaks. I can make a DJ tape using the new information with appropriate music. I can look for music that pertains to what I must study.

Naturalist

How to study:

I can use my naturalist skills to improve my learning in anything! I can first observe carefully by using my senses to watch, listen, touch, smell and maybe even taste the new information. I can record and then organize all this data into a system that makes sense to me. I might make separate lists, use a graph, collage, mobile or visual note taking to show relationships and connections between the different parts. I can follow a hunch then test it out. I can build or imagine a living model. I can think of animal metaphors and symbols for the new information to help me relate to it. I can discover how this information fits into the natural world scheme of plants, animals and human life. I can see how things have developed over time and look for growth, change and the evolution of ideas and products. I can imagine that I am a hunter tracking down the answers by following signs and footprints. I can imagine that I am gathering food for my mind so my brain won't starve. I can imagine that I am cultivating a garden or raising a crop of good ideas for the next generation.

In this section we've explored the MIDAS™ profile and showed you how to use it to describe and enrich your leadership. We then presented four ideas to introduce the potential of MI to provide effective leadership tools. Now, in Section 3, we'll get to the heart of extra-ordinary teaching, starting with the five keys of leadership.

3 Tools and techniques for extra-ordinary leadership

Use Section 3 if you want to:

- understand the five keys to leadership
- explore your current and future careers
- develop detailed personal leadership development plans
- build up your toolkit for extra-ordinary leadership
- learn to lead others and develop their potential.

The five keys to leadership

1. People smarts

The first and most obvious skill that a leader needs is the ability to understand other people. If people are to follow you then you'll need a keen understanding of what makes them tick. The essence of this interpersonal understanding is accurately reading their thoughts and feelings.

> 'The most important single ingredient in the formula of success is knowing how to get along with people.'
>
> Theodore Roosevelt

Recognizing and responding to the feelings and moods of people was popularized by Daniel Golemen (1995) as *emotional intelligence*. Understanding the differences among people, their differing perspectives and expectations are essential aspects of interpersonal intelligence. Famous leaders who displayed great interpersonal understanding include Lyndon Johnson, Mother Teresa, Gandhi and Norman Vincent Peale. Jobs that require a sensitive understanding of people's thoughts and feelings include counsellor, supervisor, negotiator, teacher and salesperson.

Case study

Coach Joe seems to have a knack for bringing out the best performance of athletes with mediocre abilities. He manages to win games with players who are smaller and less talented than his opponents. When asked what his secret was by a reporter from the school newspaper, he got that little smile of his and mumbled, 'Focus, sacrifice and teamwork'. Pressed for more information he elaborated, 'I know each of these young men and women very well. I've watched them for months as the coaches have put them through their paces so I know their athletic abilities in detail. I keep a chart on each of them, but perhaps more importantly I try to understand the person behind the performance. I pay attention to what gets each of them excited and revved up. You know, the mental part of the game is just as important as the physical abilities. They call it "heart". I look for that inner message that drives each of these young people to dig in and give it their all when they'd rather settle for second best or give up. You'd be surprised what they can do when you tune into that. The best part comes when they even surprise themselves. We may not always win, but they're all winners when that happens.'

2. Self smarts

All good leadership begins with self-leadership. Self-understanding is the invisible and under-appreciated leadership capacity. There are three key self-understanding skills: metacognition, emotional intelligence and managing yourself in relationship to others. The core feature of what Gardner calls intrapersonal intelligence is the ability to manage oneself effectively based on a realistic appreciation of your essential strengths and limitations. The ability to recognize and modulate your feelings and moods is the other half of emotional intelligence as described by Goleman. People who allow their impulsive feelings or frustrations to unduly influence their judgement and behaviour are rarely effective leaders. Inability to recognize an ineffective course of action and self-correct is often a downfall of leaders who are overly focused outward (for example, Bill Clinton).

'Man who man would be, must rule the empire of himself.'

Percy Bysshe Shelley

Stress on the job can be a killer for some people, but effective leaders know how to direct daily work and life stresses into manageable activities and solutions. The list of stress organization strategies on pages 32–4 describes stress management tips for each of the eight intelligences. Reviewing the lists for your two MI strengths will give you insights and reminders for what you can do to protect yourself from the dangers of ungoverned stress. The key is to reflect on these tips periodically to remind yourself what you can do to function at your best for the long term. Most people can handle excessive stress and pressure for short periods of time, but we are all at risk of 'burn out' if we forget to take care of ourselves and relieve the stress when necessary. These are essential intrapersonal tasks.

Famous people who displayed great intrapersonal understanding include Abraham Lincoln, Sigmund Freud, the Dalai Lama and Benjamin Franklin. Jobs that require keen self-understanding include pilot, police officer, teacher, executive administrator and counsellor.

Case study

Vice-principal, Mrs Thymes, is the first to be called whenever there's a problem with student behaviour. Nothing seems to fluster her. One day she stepped between two students who were screaming at each other at the top of their voices. She just looked both of them in the eyes with that look of hers that drills down into your soul. The heart-felt lecture comes later. You can count on it. When asked how she has the courage to intervene in potentially dangerous situations she says, 'I've seen it all. I don't get afraid until after it's over when people tell me about their history of carrying knives and guns. When a bad situation arises I don't even think about the dangers (much!). I focus on the moment and listen to this inner voice that seems to know the right thing to say. When I say that I've seen it all, it's true. In fact, I used to have a very nasty temper that got me into a lot of trouble, so I can relate. I've been there. The kids seem to know that. Maybe they sense that if I understand their anger and fear and I share it, just maybe they should listen to me. That's my opening. Afterwards, I tell them that I learned how to manage my feelings and so can they. Most of the time, they'll come around, if we just give them the time and attention they all need to learn about themselves and how to handle themselves and conflicts in mature ways. That's what we're here for – to show them the adult way.'

---

3. Communication

You might have great ideas and a keen understanding of people, but if you can't communicate them effectively then your leadership power will be diminished. There are many different communication tools available to a creative and thoughtful leader. Linguistic skill for both speaking and writing is an

> 'I have learned to use the word *impossible* with the greatest caution.'
>
> Wernher von Braun

essential tool in the leader's kit. Well-spoken words can persuade people to engage a course of action and a well-crafted email can be pivotal for clarifying a team's goals and strategy. But language isn't the only tool in the communication kit. Each of the multiple intelligences can be used to powerfully express your ideas and influence people. Good leaders keep in mind aphorisms such as 'a picture's worth a thousand words' or 'actions speak louder than words'.

Effective communication will 'stick and click' in the mind of the listener. This is the hallmark of commercials and advertising campaigns. It is rarely sufficient to have a good message. It is also necessary that your message be delivered in a way that is believable and memorable to the listener so that it will influence their choices and behaviour. 'Sound bite' political campaign slogans exemplify this idea.

'Great men are they who see that the spiritual is stronger than any material force, that thoughts rule the world.'

Ralph Waldo Emerson

Famous people who were strong communicators include Abraham Lincoln, Franklin Roosevelt, Winston Churchill, Ronald Reagan and Thomas Jefferson. Jobs that require highly developed communication skills include supervisor, public relations, newsperson, teacher, negotiator, speechwriter and counsellor.

Howard Gardner describes 'storytelling' as a pivotal communication skill for highly influential leaders. A powerful story effectively distils nuanced and complex information into an understandable narrative. Great religious leaders throughout the ages have used the telling of parables, fables and legends. National leaders are able to tell a brief story to illustrate and communicate their ideas on multiple different levels. Abraham Lincoln was the master of evoking stories that were convincing to both the common man and his learned contemporaries (and often his enemies!). Martin Luther King's 'I Have a Dream' speech galvanized an entire generation of Americans to fight for civil rights for African Americans. Gandhi's actions have inspired people around the world for generations. A story can be communicated via words as well as embodied in actions. If there is a discrepancy between your words and your actions, then your effectiveness as a leader can be drastically impaired. Leaders who 'walk the talk' are often among those who are most inspirational to their followers.

Extra-ordinary leaders are not only good at embodying a powerful story in their own lives, but also inspiring their followers by telling an important story about *them*, their purpose and the meaning of their lives. Leaders who remain followers-at-heart will be continuously involved with their community and have a feel for what is important to them. This intimate knowledge will be well received by their community.

4. Solve complex and important problems

People look to their leaders to answer important questions, solve difficult problems and resolve conflicts. Of course, the logical-mathematical intelligence is a powerful tool for dealing with these challenges. Leaders need to be able to use four related tools effectively: logical reasoning, data analysis, common sense judgement and inspire group problem solving.

It is said that for every difficult and complex problem there is a solution that is simple, obvious and WRONG. Difficult problems require logical reasoning that is multi-step, understands nuances and is rigorous. The effective leader needs to juggle multiple sources of information and changing variables. She needs to be able to organize and evaluate the 'data' and its source. Common sense judgement guides the leader in discerning relevant information from irrelevant – to separate fact from fiction, to appreciate the contextual implications for data.

Such sophisticated problem solving requires more than logical thinking, however. It is hard to account for the powers of insight, intuition and common sense in this process. The naturalist intelligence may play an unrecognized role as well. The appreciation of patterns and deviations from patterns can assist a leader in finding the source of problems that are not apparently obvious. In fact, many of the other intelligences may also contribute to the resolution of seemingly intractable problems. Each intelligence can be used as a tool to re-examine an issue from multiple perspectives and add to our appreciation of its many facets. The 'eight heads are better than one' group process outlined on page 36 can guide a leader in using the multiple intelligences to creatively re-imagine a problem and gain an understanding for new possible solutions. Inspiration can have many (and surprising!) sources.

5. Inspiration: inspire yourself, inspire others!

Ordinary leaders are needed to effectively manage the business of everyday living. But highly effective and inspirational leaders are able to bring out the best in themselves and others. They must be able to tackle important and difficult problems that ordinary leaders shy away from. To handle these complex problems will require strong logical thinking skills coupled with good common sense. Your active imagination will lead you towards answers to problems that seem insoluble to others. All of your multiple intelligences may be involved in facilitating the resolution of difficult problems.

'The real secret of success is enthusiasm. Yes, more than enthusiasm, I would say excitement.

I like to see men get excited. When they get excited they make a success of their lives.'

Walter Chrysler

Inspirational leaders are able to focus on their strengths and maximize their deployment through determined effort and creative thinking. Inspiration does not come quickly or easily. To see beyond the ordinary and mundane and then to create something that makes a unique contribution requires courage and imagination. Inspirational leaders influence others to do more and contribute more than they themselves thought possible. Where ordinary leaders see the obvious, extra-ordinary leaders dare to dream the improbable and then strive to bring it to life.

The Latin root for the word 'inspire' means to take in breath, to give life. So to inspire one's self means to give life to what is inanimate and still. To inspire others is to influence their thinking and actions in ways not thought possible or probable. It is to illuminate what is hidden or unrecognized. An inspired speech can give voice to the secret or unspoken dreams of the audience. An inspired work of art or craft acts like a pebble dropped in a still pond – its effect spreads widely in the hearts and minds of its audience.

'One well-cultivated talent, deepened and enlarged, is worth one hundred shallow faculties.'

William Matthews

How you will inspire yourself and others to move beyond the ordinary and mundane is a matter of great consequence to the extra-ordinary leader who is not content with the status quo.

Unlocking potential – something to RAVE about!

Unfortunately, there is no magic pill or spell or quick-and-easy formula to becoming a highly effective leader. If there was, then we'd all be great and distinguished leaders and there would be very few problems in the world that we couldn't solve. Instead, the path to leadership beyond the ordinary can be difficult and challenging to follow. We are too often limited in our success because of false ideas, discouragement and insufficient effort. It takes time, energy and guidance to move beyond average effectiveness and ordinary accomplishment.

It is all too easy to get stuck or off track in our leadership development path and process. Yes, it is a *process*. You may have been born with great leadership potential, but may accomplish very little without sufficient reinforcement, effort and perseverance. Too often we forget how to move forward and get out of our ordinary rut. We may have high aspirations, but the right combination of ingredients and conditions are required for the wheat to not remain merely grain. The flour will not become bread without water, yeast, heat and the baker's knowledge and careful kneading.

If you want to develop leadership abilities that people will RAVE about then the following ingredients will guide you: recognize, appreciate, value, engage! The RAVE checklist on page 53 can be used to remind you of what can be done to promote development.

Recognize!

The first step is simple. Or at least, it sounds simple. Successful people can usually name at least one person in their lives who *recognized* something special about them. This might be a perceptive teacher or a significant family member. Researchers who have studied children who rise above their deprived environments to achieve success have identified the powerful influence of at least one adult who connects strongly with the child as an essential element of *resiliency*. To this day Branton can recall that his sixth grade teacher wrote on his final report card, 'Branton shows leadership potential'. No one had ever mentioned this before. He was usually the quiet kid in the class who was not among the 'popular' students with a lot of friends. Never before had he imagined himself as a leader until this one teacher verbalized it.

'Men take only their needs into consideration, never their abilities.'

Napoleon Bonaparte

Without recognition that a small round object is a seed its potential to become a flowering plant or nutritious vegetable cannot be realized. It takes a knowledgeable gardener to recognize the difference between a brown pebble and a seed. The first step to realizing your leadership potential is simply to pay attention to what you do well and what comes easily to you. Sometimes the things we do easily are taken for granted and we assume that everyone can do this just like us.

This is the first step toward maximizing your leadership potential. It is likewise true for bringing out the best in other people – your team, students, employees and family. To pause and reflect on what someone does well and then to acknowledge this publicly is a gift that will enrich their lives and leadership development.

Appreciate!

The second step to successful leadership development is *appreciation.* Yes, we may recognize that we do something easily, but without appreciating its potential value we will fail to put energy into its development. The idea of multiple intelligences helps us to appreciate that our everyday skills/abilities are important parts of our *intelligence.* They are more than merely nice things that we do, but instead represent something vital about our thinking. When we appreciate this fact then we will be motivated and encouraged to focus our attention and effort on their development. We may find ourselves paying careful attention to the quality of music that we hear, but unless we appreciate that this is part of our musical intelligence then we may not realize how our musical sensitivity might be used to fulfil our potential. When we appreciate our thinking strengths then we can act to make our lives more interesting and rewarding.

'What we see depends mainly upon what we look for.'

John Lubbock

'A successful man is he who receives a great deal from his fellow men, usually incomparably more than corresponds to his service to them. The value of a man, however, should be seen in what he gives, and not in what he is able to receive.'

Albert Einstein

It is at this point that we may begin to think that an enjoyable hobby or pastime may have value to other people. Could I use my people skills to organize a fund-raising party to benefit my club or might I volunteer to write a newsletter to promote an important cause?

Value!

Some abilities have more value than others depending upon the situation and context. A keenly developed sense of musical appreciation may in fact be a liability to a construction worker surrounded by loud heavy machinery. The financial management skills of a banker will be of little use in the Montessori preschool classroom. The creative thinking of the abstract visual artist may be a liability in the daily work of the X-ray technician or accountant. Where does your unique constellation of abilities have the potential to contribute something of value to the goals of the organization?

To develop a student's intellectual potential in the school and classroom we need to find the value of both the individual as well as the subject area. Can we direct the artist's efforts to learn about history? Can the academically strong student develop emotional sensitivity to classmates? Can a highly practical thinking student activate his/her creative thinking in the writing or art classroom?

To fully nurture one's intellectual growth it is necessary that we publicly recognize, appreciate and celebrate both small and large steps in its development. Progress needs to be highlighted and rewarded! We can learn to do this for ourselves so that we are not completely dependent upon the rewards provided by others. Self-directed and lifelong learning requires the ability to value one's own steps that represent progress towards important long-term goals.

Engage!

Leadership development requires effort and action. Leaders take the initiative for the betterment of themselves as well as others. Your drawing skills will not improve without picking up the pencil. It also helps to find a good teacher to direct those efforts in the best direction. It can take courage to step outside your comfort zone in order to develop your abilities. The ice skater will not learn to skate backwards without falling down more than once. The manager will not know if she understands the mood of the office staff if she doesn't verbalize, enquire and check on her sense of how people are feeling.

Our abilities require challenge if they are to progress. Teachers need to set the bar a notch or two higher for students to leap over and so build skills and gain confidence. We need to know how to challenge ourselves to move one step up the ladder of skill rather than setting unrealistically

'He can inspire a group only if he himself is filled with confidence and hope of success.'

Floyd V. Filson

high goals that may prove to be discouraging. Not all of our abilities are equally well developed so we (and our teachers) need to know how to support us in managing our limitations.

If emotional sensitivity is not the supervisor's strong suit then will she have the insight to hire a second in command who can compensate for this deficit? Will she have the good judgement and wisdom to then follow his/her good advice? If a gifted artist is not a good financial manager will he have enough common sense to find a trustworthy person to fulfil this role? We all have limitations that need to be supported as we engage and develop our strengths. If our limitations will prevent the full deployment of our strengths then we need sufficient self-knowledge to do something about this.

Case study

Laura is a student teacher who has all the essential skills to be a good teacher: interpersonal sensitivity, good linguistic skills, a creative flare with practical common sense, but what if she cannot pass the college algebra class and so is repeatedly thwarted in her efforts to obtain her education degree? What can she do? Laura wants to teach science and pass her understanding of animals on to the next generation. I would counsel Laura to use her naturalist skills as a means to understand patterns behind the algebraic formulae. Laura needs to liberate her creativity and study algebra using her strongest thinking skills – understanding animals.

Activity

Something to RAVE about checklist

Reflect on your current leadership skills. Which of the following do you see in yourself?

RECOGNIZE: identify and describe strengths

☐ observe yourself in action
☐ acknowledge personality strengths
☐ describe positive habits

☐ describe everyday abilities
☐ reflect honestly
☐ provide objective feedback on positive habits

APPRECIATE: value a positive characteristic

☐ a thinking skill
☐ a good habit
☐ how something is good for you
☐ appreciate creative thinking

☐ identify the value of something important to yourself
☐ prize everyday thinking and practical problem solving
☐ how you make sense of the world
☐ identify skills as part of your intelligence

VALUE: identify what is of worth to other people

☐ nurture non-traditional abilities
☐ support efforts
☐ describe worthy products
☐ fill a needed community role

☐ identify practical applications
☐ provide valuable service
☐ extend creative thinking
☐ solve important problems

ENGAGE: activate and put into use

☐ take on challenging projects
☐ maximize a strength
☐ focus your efforts
☐ build a limitation

☐ guide community involvement
☐ manage a weakness
☐ promote strengths to improve or manage limitations
☐ find a teacher/mentor

Use the variety of RAVE descriptors to plan for your leadership development. After you have implemented some of the leadership tools, complete the checklist once more. Consider what, if anything, has changed.

Leverage your achievement

At this point you may be thinking to yourself, 'Ah, this sounds good for other people, but I'm (or a student of mine is) just an ordinary follower with no extra-ordinary talents or skills. Is there really hope that I can become a true leader?' It is commonly assumed that only a few special people are destined to become leaders, but is this true? Might it be possible for you or a typical student to develop the capacity to lead? It depends upon several factors. First, how much effort and determination do you have? Second, do you have a plan for using your strengths to maximize your achievement? Third, do you have support and guidance for finding the right niche for your particular intellectual strengths? And finally, remember that through MI, the definition of leadership and extra-ordinary leadership is broader and deeper than you may have once believed.

'Perhaps I am stronger than I think.'

Thomas Merton

Some of us are born with obvious extra-ordinary abilities that thrust us naturally into either direct or indirect leadership roles. Meanwhile, a majority of the leaders in everyday life must work with uncommon effort to use their unique intellectual abilities to achieve success. Howard Gardner refers to this as using your uniqueness to 'leverage' your achievement in spite of your otherwise average or typical abilities.

There was a radio sportscaster in Pittsburgh, Pennsylvania who had a long career with legions of fans despite having a voice that was high-pitched, screechy and atypical for a radio personality. What he lacked in radio voice quality he more than made up for with his humorous, enthusiastic and colourful play-by-play descriptions. People loved his unique and offbeat comical expressions so he went on to a long and successful career. I sincerely doubt if any career advisor would have told him as a young man, 'Why don't you go into radio broadcasting? You'd be perfect for it!' Of course, such a career counsellor would be overlooking his spontaneous, comic and folksy expressions that the sports fans came to love.

In a sense, we all have limitations to our abilities and personality quirks that may limit our full achievement. The trick is being aware of them but not letting that awareness limit our development. The questions to ask yourself (or an associate) are: What are my strengths? How can I maximize those? What are my limitations that may get in the way of my development? Can I improve them directly? Can I manage them effectively so they don't interfere? Or perhaps more creatively, can you use your strengths to leverage your weaknesses like Laura, the student teacher, used her naturalist abilities to pass algebra? Return to pages 37–8 and review the key MI strategies to enhance your work. These ideas will remind you to consider how you can maximize the use of your intelligence strengths and manage or improve your weaknesses. It is important not to let your limitations inhibit your success.

The LEAD plan

One of the main tasks of a good leader is having a well-thought-out plan with long-term goals and short-term objectives. Goal setting both for the group as well as for oneself is an essential leadership activity that sets a leader apart from the rest. Followers need to know where they are going and why they are being asked to do certain things along the way by their leaders. This means that the leader must invest a significant amount of time and energy in setting worthwhile, achievable goals and explaining the rationale and strategy for obtaining them. Of course, goal setting and strategic planning can be a shared process with the followers, but the ultimate responsibility rests on the shoulders of the designated leader. Followers want to know, 'What's the plan?'

'Before everything else, getting ready is the secret of success.'

Henry Ford

Learning to be a good planner and goal setter for a group begins with creating a personal leadership development plan for yourself. If you have a well-thought-out plan then your choices, decisions and strategies for implementation will unfold naturally. We offer a simple acronym to assist you in remembering that your development as a leader is an ongoing process that requires sticking to a plan if you are to make progress over the long term. This applies to the group's development as well as your personal growth. Every journey will entail moments of distress and confusion, just like airline pilots must often fly through turbulent weather where they may experience disorientation. During times of confusion and changing circumstances it is necessary for the leader to remember to ask him/herself, 'What's the plan? What's the goal?' Of course, changed circumstances may require a change in strategy, but having a LEAD plan to refer to will provide structure and direction. The LEAD plan will help you to describe in some detail strategies to maximize your success. Here's how it works, followed by an activity to direct your leadership development plan.

Learn

Highly effective leaders are committed to lifelong learning in their daily lives. They seem to have boundless curiosity and inquisitiveness. They view errors, mistakes and missteps as 'learning opportunities' and send this message through words and actions throughout their organization. To ignore or cover up a failure may be a bigger mistake than the original error. This is not an easy process, however. It requires a fearless attitude and a supportive team environment. To admit to making a mistake can be seen as a weakness and opportunity for another person to take advantage of in an environment that values intra-team competition over collaboration.

'Fire is the test of gold, adversity of strong men.'

Marcus Annaeus Seneca

An effective leader's learning investigations focus on him/herself, the followers and the field. The field includes both your specific activity area as well as the larger context in which you and your group/followers endeavour. For example, if you are an independent school marketing director then you must know your school's assets thoroughly and you must also be aware of the changing environment in which your marketing people work. What are the current technological advances in communication? What are the attitudes and expectations of the potential students' families?

Paying careful attention and systematic observation skills are of great benefit to the extra-ordinary leader. Learning about the strengths and limitations of one's group/followers/team members is essential to effective strategic planning. You may know well your group's goals and have a great strategy in mind, but if your key team members are not capable of implementing your plan then it will fail. The leader walks that line between what is possible and what is actual. S/he needs to know how to obtain accurate information regarding essential elements of the plan. Abraham Lincoln depended upon reports from the fields of battle in order to know when it was necessary to change generals. He needed to understand the histories, personalities and tendencies of the various generals he was considering for the highest leadership role.

'Problems are the cutting edge that distinguishes between success and failure.
Problems . . . create our courage and wisdom.'

M. Scott Peck

The third area of focus for the lifelong learning leader is him/herself: thoughts, feelings, judgements and relationships. Extra-ordinary leadership requires regular and active self-reflection. As a balance to the leader's outward focus (on people, goals, situations and circumstances) s/he needs to make the effort to shift the focus inward and be equally rigorous about self-monitoring. Many interpersonally astute leaders may find it difficult to make self-reflection a positive and growth-enhancing element of their routine, but this will inhibit their potential. The capacity to fearlessly acknowledge failures, limitations and then to creatively develop strategic management plans is a hallmark of our greatest leaders.

Enhance

The recognition of the strengths of one's self and your group/team is an essential first step that must lead to the enhancement of these strengths if a leader is to grow and succeed beyond the ordinary. Leaders take the initiative to maximize the use and development of strengths as part of their leadership plan. Whenever a problem is encountered the effective leader will first consider how to employ his/her strengths to overcome the problem. But, the wise leader will also consider how to develop a weakness (see 'Develop' below) that may be a barrier to achieving goals and objectives.

'Who is the happiest of men? He who values the merits of others, and in their pleasure takes joy, even as though it were his own.'

Johann von Goethe

An interpersonally aware leader remains vigilant in seeking out opportunities to enhance and maximize the deployment of his/her team members' various strengths. A basketball team captain sets up plays that offer the team's best three-point shooter opportunities to take his/her best shot. A supervisor assigns the emotionally astute person to the role of project leader even though his/her knowledge level may not be the best, if s/he wants the team to function optimally.

'Take time to come home to yourself everyday.'

Robin Casarjean

Here are three worksheets that describe practical ways to begin enhancing your strengths that are keys to your leadership potential. Reviewing these ideas can contribute meaningfully to your LEAD plan.

Sheet 1: Enhance intrapersonal intelligence

Be aware of your strengths and limitations and manage them in the best way to promote your happiness, achieve your goals and to develop your potential.

1   Engage in self-assessment regularly.
2   Seek out accurate feedback on your self/skills/behaviour.
3   Schedule reflection 'think time' pre- (before a new activity), parallel (as it is evolving), post- (a follow-up review).
4   Search for (dis-)confirmation for your feelings and opinions.
5   Recognize past and current knowledge/abilities/experiences.
6   Gather realistic peer feedback on your decisions and plans.
7   Seek out appropriate role models in your community.
8   Regularly schedule time for goal setting and self-monitoring of progress.
9   Enhance your decision-making skills through self-aware logical analysis and listening to your intuition.
10 Check if your strategic plans are maximizing your strengths and managing your limitations.

Creating Extra-Ordinary Teachers © Branton Shearer and Mike Fleetham (Continuum 2008)

Sheet 2: Enhance interpersonal intelligence

To think about and understand another person. To have emotional empathy and to recognize distinctions among people. To appreciate differing perspectives with a sensitivity to people's motives, moods and intentions. To interact effectively with one or more people in familiar, casual or working circumstances.

1 Take an acting class or practise role-playing opportunities.
2 Study conflict resolution and negotiation strategies.
3 Volunteer for a variety of leadership duties.
4 Practise identifying the feelings/opinions of other people. For example, watch a television programme with the sound turned off and guess the feelings of the characters.
5 Practise 'listening for understanding' without giving your opinion.
6 Participate in community service activities and strive to understand how you can best be of service.
7 Study the life history of leaders in the field where you wish to be successful.
8 Connect employees and associates (or your children/students) to appropriate role models in the community.
9 Remind people how etiquette and social manners facilitate community coherence.
10 Read a book or article on emotional intelligence.

Sheet 3: Enhance your communication skills

Effective communication is a two-way street. Good communication involves expressing your ideas, feelings and opinions clearly; and interpreting the messages, emotions and perspectives of others accurately.

'Leaders are only as powerful as the ideas they can communicate.'
(Bennis & Nanus, 1985)

1 Read or listen to famous speeches.
2 Join Toastmasters. Take a speech class.
3 Join a debate club. Observe a debate and analyse it.
4 Take an expository writing class. Build your vocabulary.
5 Study visual communication via images, graphic design and symbols.
6 Study 'body language' and 'gestural' communication.
7 Experiment with other 'non-verbal' communications:

   a music
   b architecture
   c interior design
   d environmental
   e 'action strategies'
   f 'aroma' messages

8 Study marketing and advertising methods.
9 Ask for feedback on your verbal and written communications:

   a Is the message clear? Are the expectations specific?
   b Is the tone appropriate? Is it motivating or discouraging?

10 Volunteer to tutor children or read aloud to them.

Creating Extra-Ordinary Teachers © Branton Shearer and Mike Fleetham (Continuum 2008)

There are many ways in everyday life that you can exercise and flex your intrapersonal, interpersonal and communication skills. It would be a mistake to neglect developing them just because you cannot take a formal course or class. If effective leaders are known for their *initiative* then your development as a leader will be jump-started by taking the initiative to maximize your strengths in everyday life.

The self-aware leader who is a good goal setter knows that it will benefit the group if s/he regularly steps back from active participation in the immediate tasks at hand and (as Howard Gardner describes it) 'goes to the mountain top' for reflection. It is easy to get caught up in the day-in-day-out busyness of the job and lose track of the broader perspective and deeper implications of the enterprise. Periods of such wide-ranging reflections can enrich and enliven both the leader's spirit as well as the mood of the whole group. A dispirited leader (regardless of knowledge and skills) is more of a liability than an asset to the long-term health of the group (and him/herself!). Leaders who regularly remind themselves of the purpose, ultimate meaning and value of their work can more effectively instil the group with this motivating knowledge.

Advance

Leaders keep a sharp eye open for advancing themselves and the fortunes of their group. A learning organization may go through periods of rapid growth, plateaus and sometimes retreat and regrouping. School leaders are familiar with this cycle of educational innovations and the inevitable return to teaching 'the basics'. Recognizing this cycles can be of great advantage to effective leadership. Not all situations lend themselves to forward progress, but proactive leadership keeps both its own and the group's long-term goals and values in mind. It regularly scans the landscape for new and perhaps unrecognized opportunities to match their skills/assets to circumstances that will benefit them. Generals must keep their troops moving in a forward direction if long-term progress is to be realized.

'Try not to become a man of success, but rather a man of value.'

Albert Einstein

A wise parent pays attention to opportunities in the community for a child to exercise his/her strengths for the benefit of others and so receive positive affirmation. Branton's son, Dylan, learned to use a computer while sitting on his father's lap at the age of three. When he was about 14 Branton would drive him to adult friends' homes to help them learn to use their new computers or software. He earned pocket

'Results? Why, man, I have gotten a lot of results. I know several thousand things that won't work.'

Thomas Alva Edison

money in college tutoring maths and building websites for local businesses. He graduated with a double major in linguistics and computer science.

Dylan has surprised many people because he had a grade point average of less than 1 (on a 4-point scale, where the average is 2) during his first year in secondary school. After a lot of frustration it became apparent that Branton was going to have to 'lead' him to find ways to use his strengths for the benefit of people in his community.

Develop

There is no such thing as a perfect leader. Winston Churchill was voted out of office after the war. General McArthur was fired by President Eisenhower. Alexander the Great overextended his empire leading to its demise. A winning football coach may be deaf to the needs of his star quarterback who quits the team in the middle of the season. We all have blind spots, biased perspectives and skill deficits that need to be managed. Several studies found that the decisions and judgements of even otherwise successful corporate leaders were many times only 20 to 50 per cent correct.

A good leadership development plan must include awareness of one's limitations and ideas for their improvement and/or management. Not all deficits need to be developed, however, because it may require more time and effort than is worthwhile. It is up to the leader's judgement as to whether or not the limitation will inhibit the group's (or his/her personal) progress or not. If a leader has poor writing skills should s/he put time and effort into their improvement? How about his/her public speaking? These are situational-based decisions that a wise leader will reflect carefully upon and then discuss with a mentor or other confidant.

The MI-inspired study strategies described for each intelligence on pages 38–41 will guide you in ways to use thinking strengths to memorize, understand and problem solve effectively. Career advancement may require that you complete higher education and take courses that are difficult for you. Sometimes the smallest changes in your study approach can make a big difference to the final result.

'A wise man will make more opportunities than he finds.'

Francis Bacon

Activity

Your LEAD review

Self-leadership is the foundation for long-term success as a highly effective leader. This is your opportunity to devote a few hours to reflect on your past, present and future tasks, strategies and goals. The more specific your ideas then the greater will be your chances for actual achievement. Be honest with yourself!

Learning about your leadership profile:

- Based on your verified MIDAS™ personal leadership profile, briefly describe your specific unique leadership strengths and limitations in the key areas.
- Do you see yourself as developing more as an indirect leader (in a specific field) or as a direct leader or as a combination of the two?

Enhancement:

- Which of your key leadership abilities would you most like to maximize and expand as a means to leverage your success?
- What skills can you work on immediately as short-term objectives?
- What might be long-term goals to develop?

Advancement:

- What opportunities for advancing your skill development are there in your present career/work/education that you might strive for? Or not? Do you need to look outside your present employment/situation for ways to advance your leadership career? How can you help someone else or be of service to your group with your strengths?

Development:

- What are your leadership limitations that need to be developed or managed? How can you do this in the short term? In the future?

Activity

LEAD in practice

How much are you able to use your leadership strengths at this time in your current situation? Are you taking full advantage of the opportunities provided by your job or school? Or are the chances to exercise and develop your abilities too limited to be of benefit to you? You can do a quick reality check by completing the following checklist. You can then compare this assessment with your MIDAS™ personal leadership profile and LEAD review to get some idea of where your strengths are being overlooked and your limitations neglected.

Think about the kind of jobs, activities and tasks that are involved in your workplace.

	Never	Rarely	Sometimes	Often

Communication:

- Persuasion _____
- Public speaking _____
- Explanations _____
- Writing _____
- Visual _____
- Musical or action-oriented _____
- Other _____

Interpersonal understanding:

- Listening for understanding _____
- Awareness of feelings _____
- Understanding others' ideas/views _____
- Manage teams, supervise _____
- Mentoring, teach/advise/counsel _____
- Setting goals for the group _____
- Negotiation/conflict resolution _____
- Other _____

Self-understanding:

- Manage your own feelings/moods _____
- Self-goal setting _____
- Reflection, monitoring, self-correction _____
- Self-improvement _____
- Long-range, big picture planning _____
- Other _____

	Never	Rarely	Sometimes	Often

Problem solving:

- Judgement, decision making _____
- Practical common-sense solutions _____
- Managing complex data/analysis _____
- Complicated, long-term problem solving _____
- Other _____

Inspire:

- Engage people's enthusiasm _____
- Promote creative thinking _____
- Raise philosophical considerations, purpose _____
- Address meaningful life issues _____
- Other _____

Your perfect career

If your unique multiple intelligences strengths are the keys to unlocking your potential as an extra-ordinary leader, then finding the right 'lock' that fits your 'key' is vital to achieving success. Churchill may have had what was needed for England during the fight for victory, but not for peacetime.

Finding or creating the perfect career situation is not a quick and simple task. It will take some time and creative thinking to find the right position at the right time to further your leadership aspirations. Maybe you want to reshape your existing career or make a completely new one. Perhaps you are supporting others in their own development. Either way, the tools and techniques described so far all support such advancement.

Researchers have found that many people typically will have four or five relatively distinct careers over the course of a lifetime. These may or may not entail drastic changes for you. It is best if you consider career development to be an evolving process where one position leads naturally into the next and furthers your skill and experience

'For me, writing is the only thing that passes the three tests of métier: (1) when I'm doing it, I don't feel that I should be doing something else instead; (2) it produces a sense of accomplishment and, once in a while, pride; and (3) it's frightening.'

Gloria Steinem

repertoire. Leaders depend upon experiences to bring out their best. Would Franklin Roosevelt be remembered today as a great leader if there were no Great Depression or Second World War? He rose to the occasion and exercised his abilities to the fullest to meet the challenges presented to him. How will you develop your persuasive speaking techniques if you are never in the position to convince others?

While there may be no perfect career for you at this time, we think that it is a goal worth striving towards. But, in what direction should you strive? What should be your focus? Which strengths should you leverage to maximize your chances for success? You may have some ideas about your career directions, but the following exercise will help you to clarify, expand and focus your thinking. It doesn't matter at what point you are in your career development. This exercise can be useful for secondary school students, young adults, mid-career changers or even retirement planners. The trick is to formulate your career question carefully at the beginning so as to focus your thinking at each step of the exercise. You just might be surprised at the conclusions and insights you gain along the way.

Activity

Your perfect career

When you dream of your future and imagine going to work everyday, do you think to yourself:

A = I have NO idea what I would want to do for a career.
B = I have some FUZZY career ideas.
C = I have SEVERAL clear career possibilities.
D = I have one or two VERY CLEAR ideas in mind.

My dream career idea(s): _____

a List your strongest MIDAS™ main scales and specific skills:

	Main Scales	*Specific Skills*
#1	_____	_____
#2	_____	_____

b   Review the careers related to your #1 MIDAS™ main scale.

Careers that sound most interesting to me are:

1 _____   2 _____   3 _____

Review the careers related to your #2 MIDAS™ main scale.

Careers that sound most interesting to me are:

1 _____   2 _____   3 _____

c Select one career in each of your top areas that sound the BEST!

1 _____   2 _____

d Brainstorm careers that combine your top two choices.

_____

_____

Which of these careers are most similar to your dream career?

_____   _____   None ☐

The clarity of your focus and perseverance are the cornerstones of success. Leadership development requires that you stretch yourself to progress up the ladder. If you are happily engaged as a special education teacher then do you need to make a career shift to achieve your leadership goal? Does your MI profile match with the skills of a school psychologist or departmental manager?

Activity

Your dream career

To begin: assess your multiple intelligences profile; consider your dream career.

Step 1: Identify your top two general and specific MI abilities.

Step 2: Review the list of careers associated with your top two MI strengths and mark two or three that sound interesting to you.

Step 3: Go back over the list and circle one career in each of your two top MI strengths that sound the best.

Step 4: With a friend, brainstorm jobs and careers that would combine your top two career choices.

For example, if you are strong linguistically (writing) and musically (appreciation), then the perfect career might be as a music teacher, songwriter or critic.

'Experience is not what happens
to you; it is what you do
with what happens to you.'

Aldous Huxley

Careers associated with the multiple intelligences

Musical:

music teacher   instrumentalist   singer   disc jockey   songwriter   music critic
choir director   composer   sound engineer   recording technician   manager/promoter

Kinesthetic:

athlete   rodeo rider   acrobat   jockey   actor   comic/clown   equestrian   juggler
magician   craftsperson   dancer   coach   stuntman   gymnast   aerobics teacher
physical therapist   sports trainer   choreographer   surgeon   drama coach   manual
labourer   building trades   assembler

Linguistic:

writer, poet   journalist   storyteller   teacher   manager   supervisor   lawyer
public relations   playwright   editor   salesperson   sales   interpreter   translator
librarian   proofreader

Logical-mathematical:

bookkeeper   records clerk   accountant   financial services   lawyer, paralegal
inventory control   electrical engineer   systems analyst   statistician   biologist
researcher   computer programmer   chemist   investment broker   pharmacist
mechanical engineer

Spatial:

landscape designer   interior designer   architect   advertising   navigator   artist
craftsperson   seamstress, tailor   drafting   mechanic   builder   engineer
graphic designer   photographer   fashion designer   surveyor   set designer
urban planner   cartographer   carpenter, builder   film editor   make-up artist
hairdresser   commercial artist   sign painter   furniture restorer   geographer   pilot

Interpersonal/intrapersonal:

teacher   counsellor   PR/promoter   childcare   salesperson   politician   secretary   nurse   coach   social worker   consumer services   sales   homemaker   probation officer   recreation aide   manager   receptionist   clergy   psychologist   waiter/waitress

Naturalist:

animal trainer   farmer   fisherman   hunter   astronomer   culinary scientist   forester   doctor   scientist   biologist   veterinarian   meteorologist   naturalist   -   guide/tracker   physicist   gardener

Final GOALS

The development of your unique leadership potential can begin today by creatively thinking about how you might be able to employ your MI leadership skills in the service of your community/colleagues or perhaps family. By taking the initiative and making EXTRA effort to contribute something worthwhile to other people you can make the world a better place as you gain valuable experience and skill development towards your GOAL of becoming an extra-ordinary leader!

Activity

Go for it!

What are your immediate and short-term objectives for development of one or two key leadership skills? I would like to improve my ability to:

1 _____

2 _____

Objectives:

Can you identify a few needs of your group/community/team/workplace that can benefit from your leadership? List or describe a few that you might be able to act upon.

Altruistic:

How can you take the initiative right now to make the world a better place? Not in a month, but today! Which one of your key skills can be used to do this? What are your reflections on the philosophy of servant leadership? Is it practical or not? How does it relate to your own leadership development?

Learning from failure/frustration:

Extra-ordinary leaders have all faced great failures and frustrations, but a secret of their ultimate success was the ability to sort through the broken pieces and learn something important to them. If you are now experiencing, or have in the recent past experienced, a frustrating experience or failure, how can you help yourself to take something away from this situation that will sustain your leadership development?

4 Being extra-ordinary in the UK and US

Use Section 4 if you want to:
- understand the differences and similarities between the US and UK education systems
- be inspired by the leadership stories of extra-ordinary teachers, learners and leaders
- gain ideas for developing your own leadership
- find out how extra-ordinary leaders help others to grow into leaders themselves.

UK v US education

The case studies and leadership stories in this final section come from teachers and learners with whom we have worked. They are based in the UK and the USA and to help you get the most from these inspiring tales we offer you simple (and therefore incomplete) descriptions of our two approaches to teaching and learning.

The UK

The government Department for Children, Schools and Families (DCSF) is responsible for all schooling and for educational standards in England. It delegates strategic and financial management to 150 local authorities, which in turn offer support, guidance, training, consultation and resources to their area schools through advisory professionals and outside specialists. Each school is managed by a leadership team comprising the headteacher, deputy headteacher and one or more senior teachers. Some rural schools for younger children have less than 20 pupils; large inner-city ones for older students can have over 2,000. Class sizes are around 30 and schools are generally well resourced, many having been refurbished or rebuilt over the last few years.

Education from ages 0–19 is driven by the *Every Child Matters* (ECM) strategy:

The Government's aim is for every child, whatever their background or their circumstances, to have the support they need to:

Be healthy
Stay safe
Enjoy and achieve
Make a positive contribution
Achieve economic well-being'

ECM is the phoenix that rose from the ashes of a tragic set of blunders. On 25 February 2000 an eight-year-old girl called Victoria Climbie died from a combination of hypothermia, malnutrition and sustained physical abuse. The pathologist who examined her body counted 128 individual injuries and scars. Victoria slipped through the net held by the many professionals who should have saved her: education, health, social and legal. The subsequent inquiry discovered a catastrophic breakdown of communication and the systemic failure of childcare organizations to work effectively together. There was no joined-up thinking and no coherent action. Agencies responsible for different aspects of childcare are now required to communicate and cooperate on the implementation of ECM's five requirements.

At the time of writing, a rationalization of ECM and other initiatives has just been proposed. The Children's Plan is a £1 billion ten-year strategy for education, welfare and play, including changes to the school curriculum and the possible end of tests for young children by 2009. The aim, according to Ed Balls, the Minister of Education, is to make 'our country the best place in the world to grow up'.

Entitlement

Education is an entitlement for all English children aged 5–16. It is also a legal requirement that they attend school for these 11 years. English state schools are government run and funded through the income tax levied on the English workforce. Subsidized nursery funding is available for children from birth to 3 and moves

---

*www.everychildmatters.gov.uk/aims/

are afoot to raise the age at which children leave education and training from 16 to 18*. Private (also called public) schools are fee-paying, largely autonomous and compete with each other and the state system to capture the academically brightest children. There has been a recent exodus from state to private education† by the so-called English 'middle classes' (an historical and cultural term referring to a large proportion of the English population who have high career aspirations, life expectations and income). Parental choice as to which state school they send their children is a political bargaining chip and practically unworkable. Parental 'preference' is nearer the truth. 'Good' state schools are always oversubscribed and neighbourhood house prices are very much higher than equivalent properties next to weaker schools. A small proportion of parents home educate their children.

Curriculum

The English National Curriculum was established in 1988 to provide a broad and balanced educational experience offering continuity and progression of skills and understanding. The notion of a National Curriculum was, and is, largely welcomed by teachers. But in early incarnations it proved to be an unwieldy, content-driven document. It covers the arts, sciences, religion, IT, sport, humanities, citizenship but emphasizes literacy, numeracy and testing. Aspects of the curriculum are always under review, attempting to keep it relevant to the twenty-first century. The trend over the last few years has seen it evolve to be more focused on skills and creativity. However, none of the content has been dropped and teachers continue to feel overloaded.

Children attend school for around seven hours a day, 190 days each year. They have 13 weeks of holiday, the longest being a six-week summer break stretching from the end of July to the beginning of September. This is an historical legacy from the time when all hands were needed in the fields to help bring in the harvest.

Education is organized into four Key Stages and a Foundation Stage by age as follows:

*www.timesonline.co.uk/tol/life_and_style/education/article1292132.ece]

†www.telegraph.co.uk/news/main.jhtml?xml=/news/2007/11/10/nschool110.xml

Age	Stage	Year	School	Official Testing
3–4	Foundation	–	Nursery	Foundation Stage Profile
4–5	Foundation	Reception	Infant	Foundation Stage Profile
5–7	Key Stage 1	Year 1, Year 2	Infant	Year 2 – teacher assessments in maths, English and science
7–11	Key Stage 2	Years 3–6	Junior	Year 6 – tests in maths, English and science (SATs)
4–11	Foundation	KS1 and KS2	Years R–6	Primary
11–14	Key Stage 3	Years 7–9	Secondary	Year 9 – tests in maths, English and science (SATs)
14–16	Key Stage 4	Years 10 and 11	Secondary	GCSE tests in a wide range of subjects
16–18	Further Education			A levels or a series of vocational qualifications
18+	University			Academic and vocational degree

Inspection

The Office for Standards in Education (Ofsted – www.ofsted.gov.uk/) is responsible for inspecting all educational and childcare facilities in England. A school Ofsted inspection is short and sharp. Less than a week's notice is given for a two- or three-day visit during which inspectors attempt to establish the accuracy of the school's self-perception. They compare a SEF (Self Evaluation Form completed by the headteacher) with their observations. Inspections are generally anticipated with anxiety. When lessons are observed the teacher is graded against national standards, but personal feedback, praise and targets for growth are rarely offered. This is the domain of school leadership professionals. Ofsted plays an essential role in the monitoring and accountability of those who spend 'public money' on education. It also provides data that can be used to measure progress and inform national educational policy.

Personalized learning

A major initiative of the last few years, personalized learning, runs alongside the ECM agenda mentioned above. It recognizes that each pupil is different and that teaching must evolve to meet diverse learning needs. It has five strands:

- assessment for learning
- effective teaching and learning
- curriculum entitlement and choice
- organizing the school
- beyond the classroom.

Historically, the UK's best teaching developed to meet the explicit learning needs of special needs and gifted and talented children. Schools are now using this practice as a means to implement personalized learning. Where possible, all learners are to be included in a teaching group, rather than attending a special school or being removed from class. Account must be made of their learning preferences. England is waking up to the idea that every child learns in a different way but teachers wrestle with personalized learning, often seeing it as 'yet another thing to do' rather than an enrichment in pedagogy.

Education in the UK appears to be in tension between two cultural and educational poles: solutions imposed from above and solutions emerging from below. This is embodied perfectly in the concept of personalized learning: PL is something that teachers are told to do by the government, but something that must be driven by individual learners in classrooms. Perhaps this dichotomy is a legacy of England's class system: society organized by clear demarcations of attitude, behaviour and wealth, where a small group of educated people told everyone else what to do. Perhaps it is just natural forces at work: forces that sculpt a country and its people over time. Whatever the reason, this strain between opposites explains the ways in which MI is embraced or rejected in English classrooms.

The USA

In many ways, the educational system in the USA is very similar to that in the UK, but there are a number of differences worth noting.

Historically, the federal government has played a very small role in the design and management of schools since this responsibility has been reserved for individual states. It has been viewed as 'meddling in states' rights' whenever the national government placed restrictions or demands on them. The national law ordering full racial integration of schools in the1960s that resulted in armed confrontations in some southern US states is a case in point.

There has never been one standard 'national curriculum' mandated to be taught in all 50 states with a 'national achievement test' to measure how well students are mastering the content of such a curriculum. Each state sets its own general standards and, in fact, even more specific curricular decisions are left to each local community's 'board of education'. Education in the USA grew directly from its 'pioneering spirit' where each new township or city was expected to set aside land and resources for the support of the 'local school'. Community involvement in the overall design and day-to-day management of the school was a point of civic pride.

This decentralized control over schools and teaching began to change drastically in 1983 with the publication of the influential report, *A Nation at Risk: The Imperative for Educational Reform*. This report by the National Committee on Excellence in Education is (in)famous for popularizing the phrase 'a rising tide of mediocrity' threatening America's schools. This report sounded an alarm in the ears of the nation's leaders that our schools were failing to do their jobs in educating all students to high levels of achievement.

Politicians eagerly leapt on the 'school reform' campaign bandwagon with megaphones in hand shouting about the need to 'fix our failing schools' (Vote for Me!). This school reform movement coincided with a national rethinking of the social values and turbulence of the 1960s and 1970s (racially integrated institutions, women's rights, sexual freedoms, questioning authority, losing the Vietnam War, and so on). In the minds of many (especially the social conservatives and political leaders at the helm) the grassroots educational innovations that embody 'liberal ideas' such as open classrooms, child-centred instruction, non-graded classes, and so on, came to be associated with failing schools that were a direct result of low standards and a lack of accountability to a higher authority. Individual teachers in classrooms and local control of educational standards were now prime suspects in the decline of students' test scores.

The nation's leaders were eager to assume responsibility for correcting this 'crisis in education' since it posed a challenge to the country's future as an economic powerhouse. As other industrial and developing countries flexed their economic muscles (Singapore, Japan, Korea, and so on) they were also now dominating in the realm of international comparisons of mathematics, reading and science test scores. America's industrial/manufacturing dominance was eroding and jobs were swiftly being exported and outsourced. It became obvious in the minds of our leaders that our educational 'production' systems were deeply flawed and in serious need of 'retooling'. In 1998, during the administration of Bill Clinton, the first serious laws aimed at 'school accountability' leading to the 'No Child Left Behind' (NCLB) law was passed with bipartisan support by the US Congress. This law required that all states devise a system of 'quality control' that regularly tested the students' achievement in several core subject areas.

This 'industrial quality control' solution to the problem of educating young people is viewed as the lever by which the federal government can exert influence over the educational (manufacturing) process without directly interfering in the day-to-day management of local schools. School systems and states that failed to comply with the requirements of the NCLB law would lose any federal funds for education. National leaders would use the power of the purse strings to indirectly leverage change in educational practices.

All 50 states diligently invested tens of millions of US dollars in the creation of their own tests of academic achievement to be administered state-wide. The test publishing industry flourished while manufacturing jobs continued to be outsourced to Mexico, China and Korea. The federal government demanded that all students be held to 'high standards' and achieve at 'above average' levels. For nearly ten years the controversy over the effectiveness of the NCLB law has raged. The effect of the law on curricular content and teacher effectiveness has been relentlessly studied, debated and passionately argued on both sides of the equation.

Teachers (as a group) predominately hate the law. School administrators are equivocal. Parents and community leaders are mostly confused and divided. Some wonder what the big fuss is all about. They ask, 'Shouldn't all students be expected to learn to read and do everyday maths?' Other parents relate horror stories of the devastating effect of 'high stakes testing' on their child's mental health, creativity, motivation, and so on. The NCLB law is currently (as of 2008) being reviewed for reimplementation and possible revision. The debate continues to rage with data and stories being hurled by both sides striving to answer the question, 'Does NCLB work? If so (or not), how should it be revised?'

One thing is for certain, over the past ten years the emphasis in the classroom has changed from student-centred instruction and creativity to 'higher test scores'. All student achievement test scores are published once a year in local newspapers. Each school district is labelled according to how well its students score, from the lowest level of Academic Emergency to Excellence. Schools that ultimately fail to progress on a set of 'benchmarks' are slated for closure or other drastic consequences. Each school's rating is Hot News Item #1 in the daily newspapers and television news reports. How a teacher or a school goes about obtaining those higher test scores doesn't seem to enter into the conversation very much (unless they are caught rigging the tests!). The explicit message to every single teacher in a school and district is, 'Raise those student test scores or else suffer the consequences!'

This focus on measuring student learning via multiple-choice, paper and pencil, or timed tests has derailed the implementation of multiple intelligences-inspired instruction and curriculum across the nation. MI values authentic assessment over paper and pencil tests. When *Frames of Mind* was published in 1983 by Howard Gardner it received an overwhelmingly enthusiastic reception from teachers everywhere. They loved it! As if to say, finally, a psychologist who truly understands the minds of children that we work with every day in the classroom!

But, educational psychologists (devotees of IQ theory and tests) and our national leaders who embrace the 'industrial model' of school reform were suspicious of MI and its apparent roots in the 'progressive and liberal' educational traditions of the 1960s. To empower teachers to creatively design MI-inspired lesson plans and value the practical and creative thinking abilities of students as much as their 'academic skills' were direct threats to their attempts to leverage higher test scores across the nation. Viewing teachers as curriculum leaders and innovators is now passé and discouraged. Curriculum designers and textbook publishers have raced to produce 'teacher proof' curricula. Highly structured maths and reading skills programmes have been mandated. Top-down controls are not merely trickled but flooded into the hour-by-hour classroom experience: more quizzes! more tests! are the order of the day. One preschool teacher estimates that she now spends 30 or more hours per school year in simply administering a wide (and repetitive) battery of tests and assessments. For better or worse, who's to say? It probably depends upon your perspective to a very large degree because the controversy still headlines all the educational news reports.

Meanwhile, small pockets of schools and a diehard band of MI-inspired educators continue to find creative strategies for developing students' 'academic skills' as well as enhancing creative thinking and pro-social involvements. Since the introduction of MI, other theories describing students' abilities have emerged to both enrich (and confuse) our understanding of how people think and solve worthwhile problems. Emotional intelligence is highly valued by some schools. Robert Sternberg's Triachic theory proposes that practical and innovative thinking skills are just as important as analytic/academic abilities. I refer to these competing theories as the 'intelligence wars' that have caught educators in the crossfire so that they are stymied in their desire to reform instruction informed by 'good theory'. School and community leaders don't want to hear about 'good educational theory'. Their only concern is 'higher test scores' so as to avoid public humiliation and fiscal consequences.

If classroom leaders and school administrators are to lead ALL of our students into a future that values and challenges each child's unique profile of intellectual abilities then we need a ceasefire in the 'intelligence wars'. We need a good theory of intelligence that doesn't minimize the value of academic skills in favour of other abilities and vice versa. It has been an error in our thinking to view MI as a 'revolutionary' idea that positions itself against IQ. It is an error to view MI as 'anti-academic achievement'. MI includes and embraces the cognitive skills that comprise IQ, for example logical thinking and linguistic competence. If we are to implement MI effectively in our daily lessons and school design then we need a comprehensive understanding of intelligence that integrates the practical with the possible.

Consistent with the personalized learning initiative in the UK, I have described an Integrated Model of Multiple Intelligences (IMMI) that teacher leaders can use to create enriched classroom learning experiences that value both academic accomplishments as well as recognizing the unique MI profiles of all students. IMMI uses data from a wide variety of sources to describe and validate an understanding that each of the eight intelligences can be expressed in practical, academic and creative ways (Shearer, 2006). IQ skills are appreciated as important aspects of the logical and linguistic intelligences. Emotional sensitivity and competence are recognized as valued aspects of the intra- and interpersonal intelligences. Educational leaders can use IMMI to avoid taking sides in the IQ versus MI debate. They can refer to large-scale data (Shearer, 2007) and neuroscientific studies to support their use of MI-inspired learning activities and curriculum.

IMMI may not provide immediate answers to practical questions such as, 'Should all students be expected to master advanced algebra? Should music instruction be a part of every student's school day? Are community service programmes worth the financial investment? How long should the school day be? Is it worthwhile rewarding teachers for students' improved test scores?' Implementing an IMMI-inspired curriculum may not be a 'quick and easy' solution to whatever ails a school system, but it does give school leaders a firm base from which to effect changes that are practical, research-based and supported by 'good theory'.

The five keys to extra-ordinary leadership may be advanced when the IMMI perspective is used to enhance education. The rich and vibrant vocabulary of IMMI can be used to communicate one's vision of how a highly effective school can serve the learning needs of all students (intra- and interpersonal). Complex problems and issues that face school leaders can better be explained when they are framed inclusively rather than as 'IQ versus MI'. When everyday skills are recognized as important aspects of one's intellectual endowment that have value to the community then we are all inspired to give our best efforts. This is educational leadership that will truly lead us into a better future!

My long and winding road (or a student in the school of hard knocks)

Dr Branton Shearer is the originator of the concept of extra-ordinary leadership. As such, it is fitting to describe his own leadership journey.

Case study

I was a carpenter for three long and miserable years. Understanding why I became a carpenter and the desire to help other people to avoid taking the long and rough road toward a fulfilling leadership path are the twin sources of inspiration for this book. There is little doubt that if I'd stayed a carpenter then I would never have reached above the heights of mediocrity. I was slow-witted and miserable. The best days were when it rained or snowed and we were sent home. It is no wonder that I kept getting laid off because I probably drove the other carpenters crazy with my frequent and annoying questions. You can gain a better understanding for why I was unhappy and unsuccessful as a carpenter by reviewing my MIDAS™ profile of abilities below.

$\Rightarrow$

MULTIPLE INTELLIGENCES DEVELOPMENTAL ASSESSMENT SCALE

MIDAS Version 3.2 Processed 10-08-2003 for Branton Shearer

Sex: M   Education: 16   Birth Date: 8-5-55   ID number: 2   Code: 2

The following profile represents areas of strength and limitation as reported by you at this time. This is preliminary information to be confirmed by way of further discussion and exploration.

Scales

Musical	***********
Kinesthetic	************
Logical-mathematical	*****************
Spatial	**************
Linguistic	********************************
Interpersonal	*****************************
Intrapersonal	*************************
Naturalist	*******************

The following profile represents your intellectual style. These scales indicate if you tend to be more inventive, accurate or social in your problem-solving abilities.

Scales

Leadership	*******************************
General logic	*************************
Innovative	********************

Completed items: 100%

The MIDAS subscales are listed below hierarchically from the highest at the top to the lowest at the bottom of the list. These scales are qualitative indicators of specific areas of strength and preference.

Specific Skill	Category
Written/Reading	Linguistic
Communication	Leadership
Personal Knowledge	Intrapersonal
Expressive	Linguistic
Persuasion	Interpersonal
Rhetorical	Linguistic
Management	Leadership
Sensitivity	Interpersonal
Working with People	Interpersonal
Effectiveness	Intrapersonal
Social	Leadership
Composer	Musical
Plant Care	Naturalist
School Math	Logical-Mathematical
Everyday Problem Solving	Logical-Mathematical
Spatial Problem Solving	Intrapersonal
Science	Naturalist
Appreciation	Musical
Everyday Math	Logical-Mathematical
Spatial Awareness	Spatial
Calculations	Intrapersonal
Animal Care	Naturalist
Working with	Objects Spatial
Athletic	Kinesthetic
Logic Games	Logical-Mathematical
Dexterity	Kinesthetic
Art Design	Spatial
Instrument	Musical
Vocal	Musical

The following are percentage scores. Approximate category ranks are included to aid interpretation. Please refer to the current manual for interpretative information.

Clusters	Percentage Score	Category
Musical	19.6	**Very Low**
Appreciation	25	**(Low)**
Instrument	0	**(Very Low)**
Vocal	0	**(Very Low)**
Composer	62	**(High)**
Kinesthetic	22.9	**Low**
Athletic	25	**(Low)**
Dexterity	20	**(Low)**
Logical-Mathematical	57.5	**Moderate**
School Math	50	**(Moderate)**
Logic Games	43	**(Moderate)**
Everyday Math	45	**(Moderate)**
Everyday Problem Solving	75	**(High)**
Spatial	29.7	**Low**
Spatial Awareness	30	**(Low)**
Art Design	20	**(Very Low)**
Working with Objects	37	**(Low)**
Linguistic	89.5	**Very High**
Expressive	92	**(Very High)**
Rhetorical	81	**(Very High)**
Written/Reading	100	**(Very High)**
Interpersonal	89.5	**Very High**
Persuasion	75	**(High)**
Sensitivity	96	**(Very High)**
Working with People	91	**(Very High)**
Intrapersonal	68	**High**
Personal Knowledge	89	**(Very High)**
Calculations	40	**(Moderate)**
Spatial Problem Solving	50	**(Moderate)**
Effectiveness	80	**(Very High)**
Naturalist	55	**Moderate**
Science	62	**(High)**
Animal Care	56	**(Moderate)**
Plant Care	52	**(Moderate)**
Leadership	86.1	**Very High**
Communication	90	**(Very High)**
Management	80	**(Very High)**
Social	95	**(Very High)**

I finally landed a job teaching basic carpentry skills to teenagers in a summer programme for disadvantaged youths. I loved it! I woke up early every morning and was enthused even on those days when the mosquitoes were thick and the sun was hot and the kids loudly complaining and whining. It finally dawned on me that while working with wood was good I was much better suited to working with words and people. I was 27 years old and I had dropped out of college after one year. What was I to do? My work was sponsored by a group called Project Adventure and I was inspired by their adventure activities that seemed to somehow change the lives of young people.

After a long rainy day talking with a friend who had recently completed his teaching degree via an independent study programme, I decided that would be just the thing for me to do. At the last minute I quickly wrote up my application and was accepted to the Adult Degree Option bachelor's degree programme at Lesley College in Cambridge, Massachusetts. My plan was to work part-time and study towards my degree part-time. After a year and a half of independent study I also applied for a year and a half's 'life experience credit' and then was awarded my degree in education and psychology. One morning while reading on the front porch I had vision of myself receiving my PhD in clinical psychology so that I could do therapeutic work with children. I had recently seen an interview with a local neuropsychologist who had founded a school for children with learning disabilities and was fascinated by the idea of studying how the brain influences the mind.

After graduating from Lesley College I knew that I had to continue with my education so I applied to three universities for either masters or doctoral programmes. Only Harvard University accepted me. I was rejected by Kent State University in my home town of Kent, Ohio (which is where I really wanted to go). They said it would not be a good 'fit'. I didn't understand it at the time and was devastated, but in the long run I came to understand that they were right. I would not have been very happy in their programme. I had learned a great deal about developmental psychology from my two main advisors who had both received their PhDs from Harvard and it was still the home to many of the leading developmental psychologists. So, I was more than thrilled when Harvard Graduate School of Education accepted me into their master's degree programme.

After a wonderful year of working 12 hours a day I graduated and moved back to my home in Ohio with a wife and a two-year-old son. I was jobless but holding a newly minted masters degree in counselling and consulting psychology. We were living in a rural Amish community where counselling jobs were few and far between. I put my carpentry skills to use by remodelling the woodshed attached to our old horse barn as my home office. After a long, hard and worrying job search I finally found a position as a psychology assistant doing counselling in a physical rehabilitation hospital. Here I received training in administering neuropsychological evaluations to people recovering from traumatic brain injury.

I was intrigued with how these assessments could clearly describe a person's cognitive deficits, but they didn't seem to describe their intellectual strengths. The results did not seem to be very relevant to their cognitive rehabilitation programme. Maintaining motivation during the often difficult therapeutic regime was a challenge, especially for the young men who had a hard time relating to the college-educated women who were their therapists. The therapeutic tasks they gave them to do seemed to them silly and far removed from anything they'd ever done in their 'real lives'. I'd read in the rehabilitation textbooks that we needed to understand the person's intelligence before his or her injury, but that it was difficult to determine.

One morning while showering prior to going to work I was pondering two questions and came to an exciting conclusion. First, what was it that we really wanted to know about the person prior to his/her injury? Second, how could we best get this information quickly and easily? In order to help the patient to reclaim his/her quality of life we need to understand his/her 'thinking' strengths and weaknesses in everyday life prior to injury. I decided that the most complete description of thinking in everyday life was Howard Gardner's theory of multiple intelligences. This is the idea that there is more to being clever that what shows up on an IQ test – more on this in prior chapters. I figured that we could probably get information about a patient's strengths by interviewing someone who knew him/her well prior to injury.

I hurried into work excited by this novel idea, but when I explained it to my boss he tried to talk me out of it. I persisted, however. I wrote to Howard Gardner about my idea and he responded positively within a week. I was off and running! For the next 20 years, I couldn't be stopped by criticism, lack of funding, unemployment, divorce or a myriad other distractions and obstacles. I've received rejections from every major test publisher and every book publisher I could think of to contact. Meanwhile, I self-published seven books, completed my PhD, presented workshops in eight different countries and taught a class on multiple intelligences at Kent State University for more than 11 years.

It has been my mission to create an assessment for the multiple intelligences that would help to investigate the theory of multiple intelligences as a new description of what it means to be an intelligent person. My second mission has been to figure out how this assessment could be used to enhance both therapeutic and educational planning so as to maximize intellectual development and life satisfaction. I have been blessed to travel around the world sharing with thousands of government officials, university professors, educators, students and parents an idea that started in a barn!

Needless to say, I did not begin my journey as a polished speaker or writer. It has been a continual, nose-to-the-grindstone, learning process. The truth be told, I continue to struggle with both avenues of expression. To mangle an expression, 'you can take the boy out of the barn, but you can't take the barn out of the boy'! What I lack in essential polish I strive to make up for in dogged perseverance. The second secret to any success I've achieved I attribute to my willingness to do whatever is necessary to be a good 'follower' of an idea I consider to be of great value and importance. I am willing to follow the best advice I am given to make this project successful. I have been fortunate to have Howard Gardner as a correspondent periodically throughout this 20-year journey. He has patiently read and responded thoughtfully to my numerous long-distance missives during both the highs and lows of this roller-coaster ride. He has proven to be a sustaining leader with his measured and carefully reasoned guidance. I have striven to craft my own work to the high standards that he has exemplified in his many writings.

Whenever I am in doubt or despair that I am not making progress, I stop and remind myself that it's not about *me*. I am only the conduit for an idea that is much larger than myself. My worries are temporary and fleeting. The idea of multiple intelligences is the water that I carry to the world. It is an idea that has been around under various names long before me and even before Howard Gardner reconceived it in contemporary, scientific terms. The ideas are embodied in the writings of the ancient Greeks, the Bible, sacred stories of Africa and Shakespeare. It is my dream to be a worthy link in this long chain of 'truth tellers' and I hope to inspire you to make the most of this powerful story in the creative process that is your own life so that your extra-ordinary leadership potential may be fully realized. The world will be better off for it!

US: six extra-ordinary journeys

Meet six people who hope to achieve success in life and develop their leadership abilities. Some of these people are more successful at this than others. Each has a diverse array of skills that they are struggling to fit into the fabric of community life. Everyone wants to be successful and to do something rewarding that is of value to others. Josef found satisfaction on the football field while Michelle struggles to feel good as a high school teacher. Stolli worries about finding her place in high school and Tommy is a dreamer in most of his classes except in science. Will Samuel survive with his current company and Will Vilma's student-centred innovations in her school survive?

'It is the greatest shot of adrenaline to be doing what you've wanted to do so badly.

You almost feel like you could fly without the plane.'

Charles Lindbergh

Maximum leadership growth is dependent upon finding (or creating!) the career path that will propel you forward so that you will have opportunities to actually lead others with your strengths. Listen for each person's unique leadership potential as you read their stories. You just might be surprised. Each story is presented in two parts: two descriptions separated in time. In the first we hear our potential leaders struggling to make decisions and choices about what to do with their lives. In the second we find out what became of them.

'Too many people overvalue what they are not and undervalue what they are.'

Malcom Forbes

We hope you will gain a deeper appreciation for your own leadership potential (and perhaps the unrecognized potential of others) from reading these stories. You may also be pleasantly surprised to learn that people can be *intelligent* in many different ways and that even if someone is not *academically* able that they may still have great leadership potential.

Josef, the athlete

Josef is 17 years old and he is excited about beginning his first year at the nearby university. He has been a little above average, but never a stellar student. He much prefers sports and gym class. He has been a better athlete than academic scholar. During the average school day he spends most of his time daydreaming about this weekend's football game and how well he will do. Impressing his girlfriend by scoring points in the game and hearing the crowd cheer is much more important to Josef than preparing for his algebra test. Sure, he wants to go to university, but primarily because he wants a high-paying job that will allow him to buy a great car to drive back and forth to football practice with his girlfriend in the seat beside him.

Josef doesn't think much about a future career except that he vaguely thinks that he'll follow his father's footsteps in retail business. His father doesn't seem to be too happy in his work; in fact, he often admonishes Josef against going into retail. He calls it the 'salt mines'. Josef worries a bit about his father's mood swings after drinking with his work buddies. Josef enjoys partying with his friends, too. The thought never crosses his mind to go to the library at the weekend. He finds reading to be boring and frustrating. He's always exhausted after reading, sometimes even after just a few pages. No wonder he has such a hard time finishing his assignments on time. He always seems to wait until just the last minute to leap into action and finish it up as quickly as possible. It's a good thing he takes classes with teachers who like him and are easy graders. He squeaked through algebra by the skin of his teeth. His perfect score in gym class saved his GPA from going downhill quickly.

Josef, the athlete, further down the road . . .

Josef has been elected as the president of his fraternity, which is a good thing since he quit the football team. It was taking too much of his time and he just couldn't keep up with his college assignments and fraternity duties. He probably got elected president because of his great success with several fund-raising activities. It surprised Josef how easy it was for him to design a fund-raising scheme and then talk area merchants into donating money and prizes to the fraternity. All for good causes, of course.

He talked his fraternity brothers into 'adopting' a local after-school activity programme for kids at the recreation centre in a poor area of town. Joe understands the plight of the 'latchkey kid' having been raised by a single father. He used to get so frustrated trying to complete his homework all by himself after school. The same thing was happening during his first year at college until his room-mate convinced him to visit the Academic Skills Centre. Now he has a 'study buddy' and uses a tape recorder to help him to memorize all the boring information he needs to pass his tests. What a difference it has made in his GPA! If only he had known about these tricks in high school.

Josef spends a lot of time at the recreation centre now, messing around with the boys and girls who come there. It's not all fun and games though. He's found that a few of the boys come to talk with him about personal issues after his tutoring sessions. The director of the centre asked him to lead a 'homework help group' after he found out that Josef was using creative study strategies himself. He was impressed that a 'jock' who was volunteering to coach football was taking his homework so seriously. The kids still call him coach even during the homework group.

Josef is thinking more seriously about possible future career paths these days. He'd like to continue coaching, but he's really enjoying the tutoring, too. If he can get admitted to the college of education, maybe, just maybe, he could study to become a reading specialist. Go figure. The kid who hated to read becoming a teacher who helps students to learn how to read!

Michelle, a frustrated French teacher

Michelle is 33 years old and feeling stuck. She has worked as a French language teacher in a rural high school for more than ten years. She is frustrated and sometimes depressed by her perceived lack of career advancement possibilities. Most of her salary goes towards paying her monthly bills and she can't seem to save any money. She feels stuck in her teaching position because her department head is only two years older than she is and already has her master's degree. Michelle doesn't have much appetite for continuing with her education like many of her colleagues have done. She sometimes dreams about joining a religious order in a faraway place. She finds the idea of a life of contemplation and solitude appealing. She'd spend every day reading the French philosophers and literary giants if she could. Michelle attends church regularly but not for the social or religious activities per se. She seems to go deep within herself during services as if the church completely empties of people and the minister's voice is a rhythmic bell in the distance. She's most comfortable there in her own quiet personal place. She's wondered if maybe she'd do better by going to live in a Buddhist monastery or perhaps Mount Athos in Greece, but those options generally seem to be reserved for men and very far removed from her small rural home town. Michelle is stuck wondering if there isn't more to life.

Michelle, frustrated French teacher, further down the road . . .

Michelle has discovered that her saving grace at the high school is advising the boys and girls in the literary club. They put out a student magazine of their writings and art. She most enjoys talking to those students who don't fit comfortably into the school social niches. She likes the students who are struggling to know themselves beyond the clichés and predetermined conventional roles. Other teachers think they are just confused and lost children, but she doesn't. She finds it refreshing that they struggle with words and art to probe below the surface and reveal their true and hidden experiences.

It has surprised Michelle that their literary magazine has twice received national recognition for its quality. It isn't that the students are great writers, but under her direction they don't settle for second-rate writing and artwork. They've developed an *esprit de corps* in their editorial meetings that is both challenging and supportive. It has surprised Michelle how they've more or less taken over the meetings themselves providing constructive critiques of each other's works. Of course, it took her a while to get them trained to speak honestly yet with kindness as they hold each other to high standards. It is inspiring, actually, to hear them work through the creative process together.

The students are each developing their own unique voices and perspectives. Their ability to precisely convey their intense feelings and capture their thoughts in words and images sometimes startles Michelle as if she has been awakened from a long dream. She catches little glimpses and hears fragments of herself when she was their age. Michelle is much more content with herself working at her school ever since she became advisor to the literary club.

Stolli, a budding artist

Stolli is 14 years old and finishing her third year of middle school. She's wondering what high school will be like and if she will be successful. Her mother constantly reminds her that the family has no money to pay for university tuition so she'd better get the highest grades possible in the hope that she'll win a scholarship. If not, there is little likelihood that Stolli will be able to attend even the local low-cost university. She dreams of going to one of the elite Ivy League universities so she can study art or, better yet, one of the famed art schools like the Art Students League in NYC. Another dream is that she'll one day attend film school or become an animator for Pixar or Disney. She's done some research on the internet and knows quite a bit about art-related careers.

Her mother thinks she's a silly dreamer and that she'd do better to practise her splits. Yes, Stolli has taken gymnastics since she was six years old and has been a cheerleader for five years. Her mother has faithfully paid for thousands of lessons and driven her to every try-out, practice and game for what seems like eternity. To hear her mother tell it, making the high school varsity cheer squad and going to the all the 'best parties' is the most important thing in life. 'As if!' thinks Stolli. But, she does enjoy designing banners for the school and her art teacher, Ms Mueller, has encouraged her to do more drawing.

Stolli has heard that her new high school has an art club and the yearbook uses graphic designers. Those would be cool to join – if they'll have her. Ms Mueller asked her to help design new T-shirts for the debate team and now Stolli is responsible for showing new students the right way to use the silk screening frame. Maybe, just maybe, she will do something fun in high school.

Stolli, the artist, further down the road . . .

Completing college applications is hard work! Fortunately, Stolli has a lot of good memories of her years in high school. Better than the past six years working in the crafts store, that's for sure. She must be good at her job because she was made assistant manager after six months, but she's bored by it. It helps that she gets discounts on materials, but she never really enjoyed making crafts all that much. Fine art is her thing, well; more specifically abstract sculpture is her passion. She loves going into the woods and collecting vines, sticks, dried flowers and so on and then turning them into odd and unusual objects. At first she hesitated to call them 'art' until several friends raved about them.

Stolli only has another hour to work on her applications because she has to prepare for tonight's artist gathering. She's the main organizer for this group of women who all share a passion for making art. They're having their annual open gallery auction fund-raiser this weekend. Stolli has two pieces that she *has* to complete so they can be installed tonight.

Stolli's college applications will just have to wait. She's not too enthused about them anyway. She's found it easy to direct her own art education. It has helped that her best friend, Merle, is a retired art professor and just happens to live next door to her. Merle's living room has a better collection of art books than their local library and his door is always open. Of course, Merle's taste in art is a little out of date so she tries to visit sculpture exhibits in big cities several times a year. It can be tough to keep up with the 'art world' from the hinterlands, as Merle refers to their small town.

She worries that if she gets accepted in a university art programme that her artist group will suffer. They have several young new members who have some crazy ideas about what they should be doing as a group. They seem to think that the only reason for making art is to make money. They say there's big money if you can get your work accepted by one of the large chain stores. One of them sold a line of baskets to a national home furnishings retailer and wham! She made lots of money. On the one hand, Stolli likes the idea of giving up her crafts store job and making things to sell but, on the other hand . . . Merle would be aghast and disappointed that she was selling out her art for commercial profit.

It's a dilemma. How can Stolli earn a living, attend college, be true to her vision and also keep her art group moving in the right direction? Well, maybe she'll save that discussion for her next stab at writing her personal statement on her university application form. Right now she has to pack her van up with grape vines, bent sticks and such. The show must go on!

Tommy, the naturalist

Tommy is 11 years old and would spend all of his time in the park if he could. He must pass by Fisher's Woods Park on the way to his inner-city primary school every morning. He only wishes that he didn't have to get picked up for the ride home after school by his mother. He can think of nothing better than spending the whole day in the park.

One beautiful autumn day when the sun was turning all the trees to shimmering gold he did that very thing. He copied his mother's tiny handwriting and gave the note to his teacher that he had a doctor's appointment and had to leave mid-morning. She was much too busy to examine it carefully, so he spent most of the day all by himself exploring the woods. He had a hard time explaining to his mother why his shoes were so muddy and his coat pockets were full of rocks, feathers, scat and such when he got home. When he told a friend that he had skipped school and spent the whole day alone in the small park woods, his friend thought he was crazy.

Tommy finds school tolerable most of the time, but is frustrated during science class. It seems to move so slowly and the teacher doesn't really appreciate the things he's talking about. He's all business and the lessons are like 1, 2, 3 . . . now, let's move on to the next subject. He gets annoyed at Tommy's persistent questions as if he's just trying to get the teacher off track and waste class time. But, Tommy really wants to understand more about the plants and animals they are studying and he feels bad that they have to be locked up, probed and dissected. Animals have feelings, too!

Tommy, the naturalist, further down the road . . .

Tommy thinks high school is a great waste of time. His father never graduated so he sees no reason for him to do so. It wasn't hard for him to forge his mother's signature and withdraw himself from school. He even mimicked her voice when they called to confirm. A piece of cake. He'd been in that special programme for failing kids, anyway, so it was no big deal. The teachers were nothing but over-educated babysitters. They seemed to be more interested in reading the newspaper than teaching a bunch of dumb kids social studies and other boring stuff. The last straw came when they took him out of science class so he could get tutoring to pass the maths part of the state test. He was always bad in maths, no matter how hard he studied.

Tommy laughed when they suggested that he apply for the work-study career programme. Sure, he'd worked for a long time at Jack's Chopper Shop helping the mechanics, but he doubted they'd consider that educational. He started by doing the easy stuff like changing oil and minor tune-ups, but ever since they got that computer diagnostic programme, Tommy was doing more of the mindless stuff. Tommy was a pretty good diagnostician, if he did say so himself. He'd often come up with the solution to a motorcycle's problem before some of the real mechanics. Of course, no one else knew it because he kept his opinions to himself. In fact, he didn't say much to anyone. He did his job and kept to himself.

Tommy's teachers' main complaint was that he was a 'dreamer'. He always seemed to be far away. His body was in class but his mind was a million miles away. Most of time he was at home playing with his animals. Tommy has six tanks and boxes that hold his two iguanas, three tarantulas, several lizards and a boa constrictor. This is kind of Tommy's secret world where he really comes to life. Of course, he likes being in charge of the dogs at the Chopper Shop, too. The dogs are nasty to everyone except Tommy, which is good since they're supposed to be the shop's main defence against burglars. They don't need an alarm system when they have four very alert German Shepherds on duty!

The dogs are cheap, too, since Tommy does most of their vet care. He gives them injections and everything. It's odd that he never did well in maths class since he has no problem working out the dog's medicines and nutrition. They're in tip-top shape and Tommy's proud of it. None of the other mechanics pay much attention to them so it's up to Tommy to keep them healthy and happy. No problem. They let him know exactly what they need. Tommy and the dogs seem to be on the same wavelength.

Samuel, corporate cog

Samuel has not been very successful in moving up the corporate ladder at several large multinational companies. He is a chemical engineer by training, but has recently been assigned to introduce new recruits to the company. Sam really enjoys this new assignment. Truth be told he always found chemical engineering to be quite dull. Three-quarters of his day is spent as he says, 'slaving away for the man'. Orienting the new people is easy. Make a little speech, show them the videotape and then walk them around the building. No problem. This is much better than sitting and staring into his computer screen in the lab all day. He has never been very good at prolonged sitting still. Sam much prefers to be up and moving around.

He wonders if he'll be able to keep this new assignment. In fact, he worries if he'll be with this company much longer. This is his third company in the last five years. It was a good thing that a friend of a friend already worked here or else he might not have got the job at all. The interviewer didn't look pleased with his explanations for why he'd left his two previous jobs so quickly.

The videotape that he shows the new people is such a bore. He certainly could do a better job with the dull script and selecting much more interesting music. It is a wonder that anyone stays awake during the whole 30 minutes. If they didn't have the final section on completing the forms properly in order to get paid, he doubted that anyone would still be awake by the end of it.

The best part of Sam's week is when he's playing music with his friends in a rock band. Last night after a long session practising with his band he went off on a riff rapping something like . . . 'Do your payroll, Get your bankroll, Let the jelly roll, Off your slick back, Up the fast track, Suck it up, man. Slam the time-clock, Doin' hard time, Jus' bidin' your sweet time, Hit the big time, Doin' the bad rimes, Slammin' the good times' . . . and on and on. It was pretty funny. All the guys in the band got into it. They wasted a good half- hour of valuable practice time just messing around.

The band has to get ready for their first paying gig in a long time so they need to focus on getting their groove together. He knows they aren't a great group, but it's fun and they get some nice gigs every once in a while. Actually, being on stage and leading the band is what keeps Sammy sane. He'd love to quit his 'day job' at the office and live off his music, but he knows that's a pipe dream. He's pretty good, but he's not *that* good. Meanwhile, back in the lab . . . he stretches his back, stifles a yawn and wonders how he ever let his father talk him into majoring in chemical engineering. Yeah, he always got good grades in science, but that didn't mean he actually LIKED it. It was just easy memorizing all that stuff. It just seemed to come easily to him. It's a good thing, too, because his witty (some said rude) attitude didn't do him any favours back in school. He was always the class clown who just couldn't sit still at his desk.

Sammy isn't sure what the future will bring, but his main challenge for now is keeping his head down and plugging through each workday. The weekends never come soon enough for Sammy.

Samuel, corporate cog, further down the road . . .

Samuel was pleased with how his company's annual Awards and Recognition Celebration came off without a hitch. Everyone was all smiles and seemed to be having a really good time. Even the new CEO congratulated him on a job well done. Yes, it was a lot of work, but after five years of being its chief organizer Sammy had the process down pat. Of course, over the past few years he had cultivated a good team to work with him. An event this big required a lot of people to pull it off.

Every year Sam tries to spark it up with a new activity and this year's hidden talent show worked well. He was surprised how many employees have serious hobbies and involvements other than their job. Sam leads the way with his busy schedule as a part-time music video producer. This complements his position as Director of Corporate Communications and Events, which was a new position created at Sam's suggestion several years ago. It all started when, in his own time, he created a new training video that wasn't boring. It wasn't just talking heads! It has music and dancing in addition to all the important information. Sam is proud that it presents the best that his company has to offer. He's even worked on several videos that have been featured at the firm's annual meeting and television commercials.

For his first training video he had a good time secretly recruiting a group of his colleagues as back-up dancers as his band played a 'Welcome to the Corporate Club' song he'd written. It was a pretty tame rap, but it worked nonetheless for this buttoned-down audience. Sammy knew that the first rule of performance was, Know Your Audience. Once he figured out what the company needed and how he could fill that need, it wasn't difficult for Sam to work hard to keep his bosses happy. A piece of cake.

Sure, his band still played gigs now and then around the city, but this wasn't Sam's driving force anymore. Their performances were, however, a source of inspiration for him so he didn't want to give them up completely. Maybe they didn't contribute to his retirement fund, but they did keep his creative spirit alive and that was an investment that Sam knew would pay off in dividends for the rest of his life.

Vilma, headteacher

Vilma loves her work. She has been the headteacher for a small independent school ever since she completed her doctoral studies and coincidentally turned 50 years old. Vilma's children are nearly all grown and she and her husband are looking forward to the empty nest. In addition to her teaching and administrative duties, Vilma has a secret passion.

Vilma writes teen novels in her free time. If her book club friends knew her secret identity was Samantha Sweet, they'd be shocked. But her colleagues at the school wouldn't be so surprised. She has something of a reputation as a 'maverick' among the higher administrators and the school's board. They rarely ask her to attend high society social functions for the purposes of fund-raising. They never know what might pop out of her mouth that would displease the potential donors.

Her school has a reputation that has dimmed over the years because of her new policy of admitting students based not only on their high test scores and grades. It took her many years of slow patient effort (and scheming) to institute an 'alternative path to admission'. Really, she'd admit just about any student regardless of previous grades, if the student could convince her that he or she wanted to attend badly enough. But, for the sake of appearances, she has managed, much, to her delight to allow students to submit a 'Portfolio Demonstrating Competence' in lieu of grades or standardized test scores.

Vilma completed her doctorate at an online university while teaching full-time. She was surprised how easily she understood her statistics courses that other students found so difficult. In fact, she created a web-based 'Statistics Without Tears' course that her university now offers to all doctoral candidates. Vilma thought it was strange that statistics were so clear to her after growing up thinking herself as being 'maths impaired'. She guessed that she inherited this notion from her mother who was a housewife and her primary school teachers who all made sour faces and turned a little green whenever it was maths time.

Vilma has a knack for motivating both her staff and students. Students who were not successful at other schools often surprise both themselves and everyone else while they're at Vilma's school. Even the teachers seem to have absorbed this ability to motivate some of the most reluctant of students. They don't threaten or deal out harsh punishments. In fact, they don't overdo the rewards and honours like some schools do. Somehow they finesse the best out of their students. Maybe it has something to do with the way that Vilma is such a good listener. She's also (in)famous for her witty bad jokes.

She seems to always know just the right thing to say to each teacher or over the school's loudspeaker when everyone is having a bad day. A remarkable thing about the school is the large number of volunteer organizations that students have formed themselves. Someone once remarked that there seem to be more student leaders at the school than there are followers. Vilma herself is an officer in at least three community groups and leads two student groups, in addition to some teaching and her administrative duties. No, very little grass grows under the feet of Vilma and she shows no signs of slowing down even after nearly 30 years in education.

Vilma, further down the road . . .

Vilma has just about completed the third volume of her family's history. She's waiting for a few more photographs and video clips to come from a distant relative in Europe. It has been a very enjoyable way to spend her retirement years. She retired only four years after serving as her city's school superintendent. When selected by the board she was full of big ideas and energy. She hopes her short tenure was helpful in some way.

She just couldn't continue in the position after the city's voters turned down three school levies. Her 'radical' ideas were viewed with suspicion by some of the more conservative voters (and school board members). Maybe the timing just wasn't right for her brand of innovative leadership. Her focus on curriculum restructuring flew in the face of the 'back to basics' tide that was sweeping across the country. It was a pity, but it couldn't be helped. Vilma knew when it was time to move on.

Vilma's teen novels continue to sell well and one was even adapted into an after-school TV special. That was a high point for Vilma, but maybe not as rewarding as when her former school named a new library in her honour. She spent most of her academic career at that school and was one of its star graduates. It was fitting that the library bore her name since she still goes there to volunteer. She'll do whatever they ask her to do. Sometimes she listens to children read aloud or as they give book reports. She loves to help organize the local history room. They have a nice collection of regional history books and maps. She feels a connection to the city's pioneers whenever she reads their letters and early city charters. She knows how hard it is to carve a new path in a world that is suspicious of new ideas and change.

It's funny because she never thought of herself as an innovator. She's always thought that her ideas are just plain common sense. It was other people's ideas about how things 'should be' that got in her way of improving curriculum and teaching. It's all about respect, she thinks. Too many people simply fail to respect our individual differences and each person's unique capacity to contribute to the world. If only they would just stop measuring so much and start listening with care and respect more, then they'd learn the secret of motivating people to do their very best.

Success has nothing to do with what you gain in life or accomplish for yourself. It's what you do for others.

Danny Thomas

UK: six extra-ordinary leaders

The philosophies of MIDAS™ and extra-ordinary leadership were developed by Branton in his native USA. However, they are powerful and empowering ideas that have travelled – both in his suitcase as a globetrotting educational consultant, and via print, the internet and word of mouth. MIDAS™ is now used in over 24 countries and the concept of extra-ordinary leadership is developing quickly.

When ideas like this arrive in a different culture, they inevitably undergo a transformation. Mike now presents a series of interviews made in 2007 that exemplify his experiences with extra-ordinary educational leaders, who are inspired by MI, in the UK today.

Charlotte Gormley, assistant headteacher, The Compton Secondary School, London

The Compton School in Barnet is an outstanding school according to its latest Ofsted inspection. It achieved the top grade in all 24 inspection categories. However, its pupils are no pushover. They come from a variety of backgrounds and engagement with learning is not guaranteed. In this interview, Charlotte explains the wide interpretation of 'leadership' within the school.

Mike: I'd like to think about different aspects of leadership in the school and start with your role as a leader of teachers.

Charlotte: What we did for Ofsted is we came up with a list 'wow' factors – 'what's WOW about the Compton?' One of those was about distributing leadership: it isn't just about the leadership team and the senior leadership team but it penetrates right through the school. So that actually our students are leaders as well.

In terms of us leading teachers, one of the ways we lead is by example. So there will be a number of outstanding teachers that staff are advised to go and observe – so you lead by the example of your practice. We also go into lessons and evaluate teachers' learning: you go in . . . you observe, you offer lots and lots of positives, always looking for perfection. We have sessions every year where we look closely at teaching and learning. Last year we focused on 'starters' and 'plenarys', asking, what is the purpose? . . . what is the value? . . . how do we do them? We got staff in who do them really well to lead by example. So, actually although we may lead on the concept, it's our fantastic staff right through the school who actually model the good practice. It's a shared vision.

Mike: In terms of the concepts that are to be led, do they evolve from within the school or is it imposed from outside the school? How are these concepts chosen?

Charlotte: Interesting one . . . a little bit of both I think! There certainly has to be some influence from outside school. There will always be external pressures, but I think, as an outstanding school, we look at our school improvement plan. What we're very good at here is choosing a focus that we thoroughly embed. So we will, as a senior leadership team, look at 'how do we move this school forward?' We had a strategic planning meeting last Monday where each team member looked at their area of expertise and talked about how they planned to embed that and move that forward. We tend to embed over three years, which is quite a long period of time. It's better to do this than having lots and lots of concepts coming in that aren't as good . . . that aren't embedded as effectively.

Mike: I'd like to move into the classroom now in terms of the students being leaders: leaders of learning or leaders of each other. Around the school I've seen lots of examples of you celebrating leadership. For example: students who achieved or contributed to the life of the school are celebrated publicly on display boards as being leaders in that field. But also in, say, an English lesson, how does leadership manifest in pupils?

Charlotte: We use lots of classroom management strategies to do this. For example, the learning objectives and outcomes that are written up on the board – we would ask a difficult pupil in the class to be the classroom helper, you know, kind of glamorous classroom assistant. They will write up your learning outcomes and objectives . . . or translate it into student-friendly speak . . . they do it for you. That's one level – very basic level. We also ask students to lead on instructions. You explain something, then you ask a student to explain it again but putting it into student-friendly speak which is great for less able students. There are lots and lots of kind of steps that enable them to feel that they are playing a role in terms of the leading of the lesson.

We also use peer assessment – getting them to lead on assessing one another's work so it's not just teacher marking 'this is right, this wrong'. They actually evaluate each other's work so there's a sense of leadership there too. We also have them actually leading on lessons themselves. So we have our prefects, who are a fantastic group of mature students, who go in and teach citizenship lessons to our Years 7 and 8 and literally have leadership and control over the whole lesson itself – which is a 20-minute period. We do a lot of work with them beforehand on how to do that. And, beyond that, students are involved in our interviewing process. So they will go and observe candidates . . . they will feed back to us and tell us what they think. They will be part of the interview panel. They will ask questions. So, lots of really . . . you know, we use our students to lead in useful ways.

Mike: Obviously, [there are] many diverse ways in which they can be leaders both in the classroom and outside and, from what I've seen, leadership is a quality and a skill that is valued highly here. I'd like to broaden our discussion now to different skills and qualities. I was particularly struck by one display in the school. It was your bilingual learners board, where you celebrated bilingual learners. You described one student as an accomplished artist and a linguist . . . and it was great to see the crossover of disciplines and domains there. So how do you try to value the wide diversity of skill and talent, rather than just being bound into, you know, literacy and numeracy and things like that?

Charlotte: When we were looking at positive behaviour and reviewing our behaviour policy, one of the things that came out of it was that we wanted to break free from stereotypes like: 'this child is a nightmare' or 'this year group is a nightmare'. One of the ways that we did that . . . which you've kind of mentioned . . . was display. Celebrating achievement through display was crucial. We didn't give staff criteria for their displays. We trusted them to pick out their students and celebrate what's been really successful for them. As you've just said, you walk around the school and perhaps students that are challenging, shall we say, in maths might be really successful in French or art or PE where they are using different skills. And what's really powerful about that is that it enables staff to see them in a different light. I've interviewed some students about this and one student said to me, 'You know, it's great . . . I walk down the corridor and teachers that don't teach me, come up and say "well done" and that's really nice'.

Mike: This is leading towards multiple intelligences – valuing a broad range of skills equally. I've noticed over the years that where schools have embedded it thoroughly it's less evident than in schools who are just starting out. In schools where it's deep, it's intuitive, it's implicit in the thinking and the way students and teachers relate to each other. That's what I'm seeing here. Has there been an overt use of MI or input of MI?

Charlotte: No, not really, rather than teaching MI, we've looked at how do you create an effective lesson and in that effective lesson there will be movement, there will be discussion, there will be creative reflection. So it's not so much that we've come from that theory, but that we've taken it, we appreciate how important and valuable it is, but we've looked at it from the point of view of teaching generally and infused it in that respect.

Mike: So it sounds like, that if you, if a school, if a bunch of educators just focus on 'let's get the best teaching', one of the things that will emerge is multiple intelligences but you don't need to know the theory, you don't need to go near the theory, what happens when you're doing your best by the students is that MI happens?

Charlotte: Absolutely, I think that's right. I think senior leaders tend to lead on theory. They look at what makes it work and then we break it down and we spent almost a year embedding it. With the 'starters' we talked about earlier it's not just simply 'question and answer' . . . it might be sticking Post-it notes up around the room, so we shared good practice in terms of starters, which will have covered various learning styles and MI. So it's done in that respect really.

Mike: I'd like to finish off now with thinking about you personally and drawing together these ideas of skills, talents, multiple intelligences, learning styles and leadership and put you on the spot: what makes you extra-ordinary?

Charlotte: I suppose one thing I will say is that I started as an NQT here seven years ago and I think I have learned from the best. You know, my headteacher is an exceptional woman who is not kind of interested in how long you've been in post, it's about how effective you are in post. I have gone from NQT to assistant head in seven years, which is a pretty good achievement. She recognizes potential and recognizes effective teaching so I've been learning from her. All the things that she does as a leader I hope I'm now able to do in a similar way.

Mike: OK, so what does she model to you that you value?

Charlotte: OK, lots of things, how do I summarize this . . . tough love . . . you know what we do with the kids we call 'tough love', so I know that she cares, I know that she cares about my career but at the same time there are bottom lines, so, you know, if I've made a mistake . . . which we all have . . . then I will have to speak to her about that. But what's really nice is there's a 'no blame' culture. So, I'll go to her and I'll say 'I think I may have not handled this very well' and she will say – 'no you haven't, but this is how you put it right and we all make mistakes and you learn by those'. So there's that . . . there's the kind of no blame culture, but . . . you know . . . the accepting when you've made a mistake and being able to admit to that. Her ability to be so focused and to have to deliver tough messages but do it in such a way that doesn't get people's backs up . . . I think is a phenomenal trait . . . and one I admire . . . and what is really wonderful for me here is that I am surrounded by the headteacher and seven other members of the senior leadership team who are inspirational and we work together really well. I learn every day from them, which is lovely . . . and, you know, I learn from other members of staff in the school as well. But it comes . . . it comes from the top . . . definitely . . . and works its way down . . . yeah.

Chris Neanon, senior lecturer in the School of Education, Portsmouth University

Chris is an experienced teacher, advisor and university lecturer. She is a national expert in the teaching of dyslexic learners and designs and runs courses for classroom teaching assistants. Her use of MI with special needs learners has evolved over the years and now forms part of both the content and delivery of her university teaching.

Mike: We're going to discuss the use of MI at tertiary level – both Chris's understanding of it and the pros and cons of using it with the students. Tell me first about your understanding of multiple intelligences theory.

Chris: My understanding has been gleaned variously from Howard Gardner books, listening to him, talking to colleagues, seeing it in practice in schools. So my understanding of it, I suppose, is very much at a practitioner level because that's where it's come from – although I appreciate the theory behind it. Though for me it is another tool in my teaching toolbox. I ask myself: 'Would it actually help me to get ideas over to students? Is it then something that I can be teaching them to take forward to using with the students that they work with?'

Mike: So, as you see it, MI is about how you can deliver the content you have to, but also how you can empower the people with whom you're working?

Chris: Yeah and it fits, it fits very much within an existing framework of multisensory approach, which I think has been the dominant approach really throughout my teaching career – working in learning support. MI recognizes straight away that everybody has a range of different ways of learning and the MI approach, I think, has just dealt with this in perhaps a more sophisticated and more wide-reaching way. So, when you're looking at doing things in a multisensory way and people have been just thinking about, you know, kinesthetic approach or visual approach, MI just gives you more ways into learning than you might have had before.

Mike: So, in a way, it's sort of an enrichment of what people do already?

Chris: I think it's an enrichment of what is good practice already. I think that whatever level you're working at, there needs to be a recognition that, although we use all of our brains all the time, people do have preferences and areas . . . ways of learning where they just feel more comfortable. Now, as a teacher, I think part of my job is actually to push people out of their comfort zone sometimes and to get them to engage in ways of learning that are perhaps not their most comfortable. As a practitioner, I need to recognize that I'm very comfortable with doing lots of visual things but that may not be appropriate for others. So it's not just about pushing my students out of their comfort zones but also stretching myself as a practitioner. So it works on those two levels.

Mike: So, on those two levels it would be interesting to think about practical examples and, maybe, differences in the way your students respond to not only your presentation of the theory but the practical activities which you share with them – either to give them content or for them to take away. So I guess the question is, in practice what response do you get?

Chris: Response from the students is really quite interesting because they start off with being fairly resistant and having some fairly stereotypical impressions of what they think education at university level is going to be like. They think there's going to be a lot of people lecturing. So we get them out of that quite quickly by getting them up moving around, talking to other people and thinking about issues in other ways. The aspect of MI that I think is really powerful is where you may be looking at quite a difficult concept, but you're able to approach it through a practical way.

One of the things that we do right at the beginning of the course is something which we've called vaguely 'the eggsperiment' which is to try and engage students into thinking about when they undertake a task, what are some of the things they're using. What are the skills they already have? How do they engage in that task? We ask them to create a carrier for an egg that they are then going to drop from a height and they actually find it very difficult because they think the success or failure of the activity is about whether or not the egg breaks. But actually the egg is irrelevant because what is relevant is getting them to talk to each other, to reflect on their own practice, to actually engage in practical activities in order to get underneath what it is that they use in order to learn.

Mike: It sounds like rather than just hitting them with the theory and expecting them to understand that, your entry point is through a problem to solve. It draws out of them their existing skills and enables them to reflect on what they have, and maybe other people have, and they don't?

Chris: The problem-solving aspect of it is really quite critical for the students because what we're able then to do is use their own practical experience. They are mature students – they have a wide range of practical skills. They're very skilful in their job – what's new to them is being in an academic environment and I think MI's a really useful way of getting them to cross that bridge really between the practical and the academic – to begin to recognize that the skills that they have in the practical world can still be applied to an academic world, but just in a different way. So, you're going into their learning just from something that they actually know and feel comfortable with and using MI to scaffold that. I do teach MI as a one-off lecture. We spend a day on it. I tell them the theory behind it and I get them to do some practical activities and then ask them to think about how they are going to apply that in the classroom. But more importantly for me as a teacher is the MI approach. I'm not always saying to the students 'we are doing this in an MI way' because it's the scaffold and the way in which I'm working.

Mike: It sounds to me it's a very implicit way of using MI . . . it's not an explicit 'here's the theory, let's use it' . . . you draw them into it? Once the experiment, the first activity's over with and you've delivered MI, is it . . . does it continue to be a theme throughout? Do you keep referring to it? Deliver further lectures about the theory? How does it progress practically? And once your students are in schools how does it work there?

Chris: Every unit on our course is in some way separate, it's a separate topic . . . but, from another perspective, every unit builds on the unit that's gone before. So, I wouldn't say that I explicitly say to students 'Right, OK, you remember that time when we did so and so – this is how it applies here.' However, in a more informal way I'm doing that all the time, and when students start talking about their school practices and how their teaching has changed, without fail the MI bit is the bit that comes back for them as being an aspect of the course that has really opened them to different ways of thinking about their support for children.

Mike: That's interesting to know. To change someone's mind in terms of what they think about intelligence and skills and talents can be quite a tricky thing to do.

In my experience of multiple intelligences a lot of people resist it strongly because there's a perceived attack on traditional intelligence. So you're saying that a lot of the students, they actually re-frame, consciously or unconsciously, what they believe about intelligence?

Chris: Absolutely – I think that is really so true for our students, but I think it's probably because the sorts of young people they're working with are those who struggle with their learning and, for me, the whole MI approach seems to be geared towards learning support. Suddenly you are saying to people 'you do not have to excel in the conventional ways' and actually you can excel in a whole range of ways. You don't just have two ways in which you can be good . . . you know if you don't succeed in those, there are actually lots of ways that you can get kudos, praise, acknowledgement for what you're good at even if you can't string a sentence together.

Mike: It sounds like a very convincing argument for thinking and learning with multiple intelligences. I'm also interested to know at the other end of the spectrum, are there students you have worked with who either don't get it for certain reasons or resist it or insist on a more traditional understanding of intelligence?

Chris: I haven't found anyone who's resisted it. I think, on the whole, they're fairly open and they have seen the consequences of only valuing young people if they can achieve in numeracy and literacy. And they really are at the coalface in doing that. Some of them have come back and have been challenged. They are saying, 'Well . . . you know . . . you're saying this Chris about MI . . . we can see how it works and we know how it makes us feel but actually that's not real life in schools.' So they're changing their practice when they're working on a one to one with children or in a small group situation, but what they're not able to do (and that may be because of their status in the school) is change the system. They are recognizing children by saying 'you are really fantastic working in a group' or 'you are really listening to other people' or 'you know you are fantastic out on the football field' or whatever. But they feel that within the formal framework of school those children will still be written off because they haven't succeeded in their SATs test or their GCSEs.

Mike: You're working with teaching and learning assistants, and the interesting point there is that for any gain you may make with them here in terms of thinking about multiple intelligences, there's a chance that it can be lost once it gets into the wider educational picture. What I'd like to turn to now is what you believe is the place of multiple intelligences in English education as it stands in 2007 . . . is there a place . . . should there be . . . can anything happen to make multiple intelligences infuse into what already happens?

Chris: It's about attitude change. There is nothing in the idea of intelligence existing on multiple levels that is contrary to good teaching practice. So theoretically there shouldn't be any reason at all why this isn't going on and, you know, there are so many different ways and there are lots and lots of books to help people to do it. For example ways in which you can say 'How am I going to assess this through MI?' I think there still is a need for some way of having a standard that is recognized for employers. The GCSEs have their place but in terms of teaching – how do we teach . . . how do we get children to that place – that's the strength, I think, of MI.

Linda Marshall, vice-principal, Bradford Academy, Bradford

Linda excelled as a teacher of RE before leaving the classroom to lead a major independent training company – Critical Skills. Now she's back in school managing one of the UK's newest academies. Not only is she an effective teacher and leader, but a learner too – she plans to take her GCSE maths exam, attending lessons alongside the students.

Mike: Could you to describe your role in terms of leadership and what you're hoping to achieve at the academy?

Linda: Strategically I'm second in command should Gareth Dawkins, the principal, not be here. I'm here to support the work that he's doing and to help him implement the mission, vision and values of the academy. Strategically, in terms of leadership, my role is learning and teaching and staff development. So, I spend a lot of time working with colleagues on how to improve the quality of their practice, on how to embed high-quality learning experiences for our young people and to ensure that the practice that they are doing is fully supported with a quality staff development.

Mike: I've seen you in action . . . leading . . . I'd like to hear from you though . . . what you believe your leadership style is – and maybe some examples of how you put it into practice?

Linda: I do it intuitively. I treat adults as I treat all learners and so I guess I have adopted the same style with my teams as I have done in my classroom. I like to work collaboratively with colleagues. I like to empower them. I like to get them 'on board'. I like to ensure that I know them, that I value them and that I understand them. This is the philosophy of the academy. I can do authoritative if I need to do, but I do try to be a 'guide on the side' in terms of finding out what the strengths of somebody are and how to move them forward, so I use assessment for learning techniques in a lot of the work that I do with colleagues. I try to model the behaviour that I would expect to see and then debrief with them why I have behaved in a certain way. I coach colleagues a lot. I work alongside them and watch what they are doing and give them feedback. If I need to instruct colleagues, I will do, but I use that rarely. I prefer for them to come to a decision about how to behave by their own experience rather than for me telling them what to do.

Mike: It seems like that's a very powerful way and an effective way of leading. We're working with the staff on MI today. What plans do you have for taking it forward? What potential do you see?

Linda: The premise, the basis of the academy, in terms of its mission, is that every learner is affirmed; is formed and is helped to achieve. So, affirmation, formation, achievement are at the heart of what we do. We've interpreted that as 'every learner known, valued, understood'. Now, patently, if we are to know our learners well in order for them to be successful, they need to know how they learn . . . and how they are smart. So I see MI as being a fundamental piece to our jigsaw to affirming all our young people. The area of Bradford that the academy serves is one where there is significant deprivation. Fifty per cent of our young people have free school meals. We have 26 students who are in wheelchairs. We have significant numbers who have special educational needs. But 50 per cent of our cohort are the national average and above and have not necessarily been served well in the past. So we need to make sure we raise the bar for all our learners and we help them to understand how they learn and how they can be successful.

The development of MI consistently across the academy is a major goal and lies at the heart of our learning and teaching policy. In terms of leadership our premise is that all learners are known, valued and understood and that includes every single person that sets foot in this building, that is all of the teachers, all of the associate staff, all of the senior leadership team up to the principal and including the governors.

I think that the best way to improve your own practice and your own interactions with other people is to be reflective and to think about how we learn, how we are smart and to make best use of that. We've got a tremendous resource in our academy, which is obviously all the adults in the academy . . . and, of course, the children . . . but you know, if I'm focusing on the staff, we've got lots of staff who are incredibly smart and I want to make sure that we make the best use of all the talent that we've got here . . . that we actually affirm our colleagues. Half of the colleagues have come to the academy from a school that had been unsuccessful for lots and lots of reasons and their aspirations and talents need to be raised and shared and honoured and affirmed so that they can be good at their jobs. Nobody comes here to be bad at their job. They all want to be good. So it's my job to help them to see that and MI will help me to do this.

Mike: Gardner says, in terms of leadership, that there are two distinct sorts. I think that you've described both already. I just want to clarify this. He will cite direct leadership, the 'I am in charge. I am a direct leader of you, I tell you what to do' . . . and then the one that often gets missed which is indirect leadership. For example, you may only be an NQT but your indirect leadership skill is that other people are looking at you to see what to do. They follow your example rather than your directions.

Linda: Again, relating it to the classroom, when you're introducing something new, and, of course, when you're opening an academy . . . it's all brand new – staff do want direction, they do want direct leadership because they want security – the building's new, half the staff are new, we've not worked together, the systems are new, the uniform's new. Everything's new. So they want direction, they want security and therefore, using a direct leadership style in that sense is important.

But at the same time you can't have direct leadership and always get ownership and, so, as we progress as an academy, we have to move very quickly to a place where there's indirect leadership. The staff need to actually 'own' what's happening and have had their voices heard. And the best way to do that is to involve colleagues, wherever possible, in solving the problem together. So, rather than trying to always think strategically 'that this is what we must be doing, and this is how we should do it' we hand it out as a problem for colleagues to solve. So there've been a number of occasions this year where, instead of me acting as a direct leader, saying, 'we're doing this', what I've said to colleagues is 'here's the problem, solve it' and actually some of the best ideas have come from learning assistants, have come from associate staff, have come from people fairly new to the profession. Them actually seeing their ideas working in the academy has been very powerful. And, of course, by doing that you're modelling what the classroom is like. Sometimes it's direct teaching, sometimes it's indirect teaching in the form of facilitating and sometimes it's just modelling. If staff can actually experience that in their day-to-day dealings with leadership hopefully they'll start to do it in their day-to-day dealings with young people. Some of the most powerful work we've had in the academy has come from the learners and come from student voice and the more we can model that with the staff, the more we'll get the academy that we're dreaming of.

Mike: That's wonderful to hear. Any further comments about leadership here?

Linda: I think that some people see indirect leadership as a weakness and that's a sad indictment really of society . . . that they perceive leadership as being one style but, just as in a multiple intelligences classroom, one style doesn't fit all. And, so, the tension is always between being directive and authoritative, and being more conciliatory and involving colleagues in decisions and there's a fine line between the two. It's important that we know that there are some times when direct leadership is the right thing to do, for example the building's on fire – you don't want to have a discussion about how to get out, you want direction . . . yeah? But when you're looking at, you know, developing a whole-school ethos on learning and teaching, you don't want to see that just through one lens, you'd want to bring and develop all the expertise.

Celia Walker, gifted and talented coordinator, Solent Junior School, Hampshire

Celia is an experienced primary school teacher who has kept her teaching fresh and innovative over a very successful career. Using MI, Celia is sharing her skills in teaching gifted and talented children across the whole school.

Mike: You're at the beginning of a several year project to infuse MI into your junior school. May I start with your understanding of the multiple intelligences and therefore how you think they could be useful in school.

Celia: People have different areas of intelligence where they either excel or don't. So, in terms of school, we'll be using it because at the moment we only use one or two of those intelligences in the majority of our teaching and the children's learning. We want to enable the children to work at something that they are good at, in terms of musical, or artistic or physical and so on. We feel that we are going to have more success, not just in tests but in making better rounded children.

Mike: So how can the idea of multiple intelligences sit alongside the English exam system? Do you think they can both exist at the same time?

Celia: Of course, yes, and we feel that in our school, particularly writing and creativity is a real weakness, and therefore by following programmes which include multiple intelligences we're going to increase the creativity of children, which in turn will increase their writing.

Mike: What about the staff you're working with and your leadership style to get them on board?

Celia: We have a varying range of motivations from the teachers. There are some teachers who are set in their ways and they don't think they want to take on any more. But the majority of teachers here are quite enthused by the idea, mainly because they can see a number of children in the school who are being missed out by the system at the moment: it doesn't actually help them to achieve their potential, because it's too much based on mathematical and linguistic abilities. So as far as getting people on board, I do tend to have good interpersonal skills and people do respect me and know that I'm not going to be too pushy. We'll take things step by step and I'll be there learning alongside because I'm certainly not an expert. I will be a point of reference and I can go, perhaps to experts for some guidance to then pass it on to members of staff.

Mike: This sounds more of an indirect leadership style than a direct one? Would you say that's true – you're sort of setting by example, rather than telling?

Celia: Oh yes, definitely. Our staff can't be told. They have to feel that they are on board with all the ideas and feel that they have some ownership of it, which is absolutely fine. I'd feel the same. The head has obviously sanctioned this so it's something that we're going to do. So she's had the direct input there, but my role is a sort of guidance and supporting role.

Mike: It sounds very exciting where you're headed. Where do you think it will end up in say two or three years' time? What would you like to see happening in the school?

Celia: I'd like to see a school where pupils are enthused by learning; a school where pupils achieve, not just in the tests, but in every single area that they can possibly achieve in. I'd like to see teachers more enthused and motivated and basically a happier, more rounded environment than we are in at the moment.

Mike: Thank you – that's a very good distillation of where you are and where you want to go. Is there anything else you want to say or add about our topic today?

Celia: Only that I think it's a really exciting thing to embark on. You can get really stuck in your ways: it's very easy to keep churning out the same old things week after week, year after year, but inevitably we get stale. I feel this is a new challenge for me and I know other members of staff are looking forward to it as being something new and fresh that they can get their teeth into. It's going to make a difference.

Joe Burns, associate principal, Unity College, Northampton

Joe has taken a MI philosophy to heart in his teaching and leading in several schools. He cites it as part of the reason for improved exam scores and now visits neighbouring schools to share his work.

Mike: Joe, I'm interested to know how you've used MI in your schools.

Joe: If I go back to when I first started to really come into contact with the whole concept of multiple intelligences I was vice-principal at an upper school in Leicestershire: the school was in special measures and had been in special measures for the best part of two years. We had reached a stage where teachers were teaching competently but safely and students were still very much passive learners. And we had been informed by HMI on our latest visit that we needed to do something to change that to make students more engaged in the learning process and to encourage and enable our teachers to take more risks.

I was then introduced, by a colleague from the local authority, to the whole concept of multiple intelligences and I did a little bit of work and some analysis. We analysed the students learning styles and the staff's learning styles before Christmas and really started things going in terms of looking at students as different types of learners. We discovered that a lot of our students for example were very kinesthetic and they needed to have those activities written into the lesson planning. We discovered that many of them needed to work with sound and as collaborative workers. They benefited very much from having dialogue in lessons as opposed to being kept in a more rigid environment.

After the Christmas, if I remember correctly, you came and did a session with us, with our staff – an after-school session, a two-hour session, which was very successful. And we then, as a senior leadership team tasked our teachers to prepare for a lesson observation within a fortnight where we would be expecting to identify strategies – multiple intelligences strategies – relating to the strengths of their groups, in accordance with the analysis that we had carried out. We managed to link this to the school data system so staff were able to identify very readily what particular students had what particular strengths.

We carried out our series of lesson observations and they were very successful: we saw a great deal of different types of learning activity taking place; students more engaged and there was a real dialogue going on between students, between staff and students and between staff and staff about how they learned. HMI came along a short time afterwards, observed our teachers over two and a half days, and the school came out of special measures. They said that they'd seen this improvement in the quality of teaching and learning and in particular they'd seen the disappearance of the lag between the level of teaching and the level of learning. So we were absolutely delighted with that.

Mike: So in terms of you coming out of special measures, what impact, or what part did multiple intelligences play in the whole suite of things you were obviously doing to succeed that way?

Joe: We'd worked very hard in getting the basics right. We had had one or two changes in teaching personnel. We'd worked very hard on the need to develop positive attitudes to learning, developed self-esteem in students – get all those things right – but we'd reached a plateau and we weren't making any further progress.

We had students whom we knew had ability but weren't tapping into it or it wasn't being tapped into by teachers. There was a certain degree of a feeling that they were getting an uninteresting and boring diet – substantial but not necessarily very enjoyable; not very tasty. So we were able to bring more of a mix into teaching and learning – multiple intelligences – the whole theory gave credibility to the idea that actually there is more than one way to skin a cat in educational terms and so we were able to show this practically.

I always remember going through the analysis with staff, taking note of their learning styles and then going back to them and saying, 'Have a look at your learning style – you're very much a (and we'll use the simpler terms) word learner or a number learner. Now look at the analysis of your groups. Who are you preparing the lessons for? You or for your students?' The lessons were being prepared to the teachers' strengths and not the students' strengths and that penny dropped. There was a realization that this was what they needed to do.

Of course some people, for example in technology and the art departments said, 'Told you so! This is what we do anyway because we are this type of learner ourselves.' But for many others it was a real new dawn in terms of how they approached learning. What was most interesting was that some of the most secure teachers took this to heart. One outstanding teacher – a lady who retired a year or so afterwards and had been teaching at the school for 34 years – said, 'Great! I can do something else with my students.' And so her lessons just went up to another level. But other teachers were able to see the most credible members of the school – teaching staff, practitioners – embracing this whole concept, applying it to their own lessons and reaping the benefits and getting the results. And that as much as anything else helped to embed it in the practice of the school.

We did the practical things like we changed the lesson plans to identify the multiple intelligence strategies used within this lesson and that's something we've done in my current school, but it's not quite at that stage yet. And this was very important because it flagged up to anyone working in the school or who came to observe a lesson that we took this seriously. Stuff was up and around the school. We had the posters and all the bits and pieces; we changed the planners – the school planners so that they included multiple intelligences and individual pupil profiles. They could refer to it, they had all that evidence and they were able to tell you, say months later, 'I'm this type of learner and I know about it.'

Subsequently, as I said, the school came out of special measures. At that time the results were in the low 40 per cent for 5 A*–C. Two or three years down the line it's now 67 per cent 5 A*–C in 2007. That's a very significant upward trend and I believe that the work we did with multiple intelligences has contributed greatly to it because it has been about raising awareness, raising expectations and an understanding that there are different strategies that we can use to tap young people's potential.

Mike: As an educational leader, you've obviously had great success using MI as one of the things in your leadership kitbag so to speak. I'm interested now that you've moved on to a different school to think about multiple intelligences and leadership and possibly how you use the multiple ways of thinking and learning in strategic management, in day-to-day contact with people and also in terms of getting MI into a new school.

Joe: I think as a school leader what I've done is I've taken this to this school, Unity College, but I've been the one who has stood up at the front and led it on. And I've started with the staff and have worked on the students and if you visualize the presentation I use which features *Simpsons* characters (of which I'm Mr Burns) it does get a certain reaction from students and staff. But that's all part of the engagement process and that's not something I have an issue with so we can get past that very easily.

We've talked about credibility. There has to be credibility; somebody with status saying to colleagues, 'This is what you need to do, this is why it works, these are the benefits' and somebody saying the same to students. And what's interesting is that students are actually saying, 'Ah this is about me as an individual, not just as a statistic, or part of a cohort, but actually me as an individual – how I learn.'

Now what I feel is that my current school isn't yet at the stage of my previous one in the application of MI. I think we've had a go at it but we've had a turnover of staff. This school is in a category as well and there have been perhaps more issues that we've had to deal with but, however, we do now have a sound base of staffing. We have some exceptional teachers who are very capable practitioners and who are ready to run with this more effectively. I think we will continue to build on what we have done and as a school leader I will be passing on this message to all and sundry that it will and does make a difference.

My bosses are concerned about results, about outcomes, and I can quote the evidence that says MI will impact on results because students become more engaged in their learning; they are less likely to switch off and misbehave and they will produce a higher level of outcome than they would do otherwise. So that's a very powerful message to get across and once people hear that and understand it then they do support it.

I think that strategically at the school my role is very much focused on teaching and learning, curriculum and that sort of thing. I'll be quite frank and say that I am by no means the best practitioner that I've ever seen, but it doesn't mean to say I don't know a good idea when I see it. And I see the difference MI makes to colleagues' practice and in students' learning. I think that in whatever school I work in, I would want there to be a real emphasis on the need to engage all the multiple intelligences and to develop a wide range of strategies to address all the learning styles of the students.

I've presented multiple intelligences work to two high schools, a primary school, local authority groups in my last area on a couple of occasions and it's always been very well received. And I know there's been follow-up certainly in the two high schools, who took it on for themselves. They'd probably had enough of me and wanted someone else to do it! It was very interesting because the one school in particular said the same thing – we've reached this plateau – and our kids are getting switched off – we need to do something else. This is what we're bringing along to it. I know that there is a great market for it.

We're very keen to develop the Year 7 curriculum more along a primary model. I'm very much about developing our children as confident independent learners. And very often we feel they leave primary school with these skills but the secondary school curriculum in this set-up inhibits that instead of developing it. And we want to change that around so MI will play a key part in that for this school in the future and that's certainly where we plan to go.

Eric Pearson, mathematics teacher, Bradford Academy, Bradford

Like Linda (above) Eric works at the Bradford Academy. It's because of the school's leadership ethos that Eric feels empowered to go beyond simply turning up for work each day.

Mike: Eric, could you tell me a little bit about your own experience of school when you were a child?

Eric: As a young boy aged six, I was learning to do subtraction – take-away – borrows – I couldn't get them right and used to get my hand smacked with a 12-inch ruler for every one that I got wrong. That was a lot of hand smacking.

Mike: It sounds like the teacher had a pretty interesting teaching style. How did she try and teach you maths?

Eric: Just by modelling the process.

Mike: How do you try and use MI, based on that, with the kids with whom you learn now?

Eric: In maths I use a lot of linguistic techniques; make sure that the students understand the words that we're using to convey the concepts. The words are important. They can use the words and the words are meaningful. Another way is kinesthetic – manipulating objects, comparing and contrasting, putting things into groups, looking at the odd one out and trying to justify and use a technique where every one can be the odd one out – doesn't just have to be one of them.

Mike: From my point of view it's rare to come across a mathematician or scientist who's an advocate of MI. You actually put that to good use in a website that you're developing.

Eric: The intention is to hit every objective in the National Strategy at Key Stage 3 that is in the Year 7, Year 8 and Year 9 teaching programme covering levels 4 to 7. I'm designing an e-learning package that provides wherever possible the various learning styles accessing each topic: every piece of text that appears on the screen is also spoken. So you just turn the sound on and you can listen to it. Whatever learning style is applicable to that topic will be used in every lesson. There's a lesson section, a practice section and an assessment session and that covers the whole range of Key Stage 3.

Mike: And it's set up so that its entry point is through a Mind Map®?

Eric: If you can imagine looking at every objective over Key Stage 3 there's a mass of links there. So to simplify it what I've done is to use Tony Buzan's i-map software to create a Mind Map® of the National Curriculum and the National Strategy. The branches of the map have hotspots in the image. If you move the mouse to the branch, you get a little window that pops up just there to describe what you'd see if you went to that page, click it, and then you very rapidly get to the lesson or the practice session or the assessment for any topic that you want.

Mike : It sounds fascinating – lucky students who eventually get to use that. We were talking earlier about one of your success stories – one of your students using a different piece of software – Speech to Text – can you tell me a bit about that student themselves in terms of their esteem and what you managed to do with them?

Eric : It was someone who has severe dyslexia and through the lack of ability to read his ability to write is impaired as well – seriously. I introduced him to Speech to Text – a facility that's built into Word and I've been working with him to train the voice recognition of Word to his voice and all he has to do is put the headset on, start up Word and speak and the words appear on the screen for him.

Mike: And what have been the changes in terms of his attitude and esteem after doing that?

Eric: When I first suggested this to him his response was that his jaw dropped and he offered to shake hands with me. And he said, 'If I'd have had this last year, all my stories would have been in print now.'

Mike: Brilliant. I'd just like to finish off if I may with a hypothetical question. You've obviously got a lot of interest and understanding of learning styles, multiple intelligences and you're putting that to some valuable practical use using technology.

If you could go back in time to your mathematics teacher who used the slates and the sticks, what would you want to say to her?

Eric: I'd say don't teach me mathematics. Teach me how to learn mathematics. I don't go into a classroom at all nowadays to teach mathematics. I go to teach my students how to learn it.

Conclusion

Yes, every long journey begins with the first step. Of course, you've already taken many steps in your own leadership development so the question now is: What will be your NEXT best step? What will you do different tomorrow morning? How will you wisely use your time? Will you choose to focus your extra time and energy on improving a particular skill that is a strength for you? Will you find a way to use this skill in your current workplace? Or will you need to volunteer in a community organization to exercise this skill in a leadership role?

Maybe you will decide to improve a limitation like a fear of public speaking. Maybe you can work on ways to better manage your temper, budgeting or time management. Would it help you to read up on dealing with difficult people? Are you a good negotiator? These are good questions to ponder as you discuss your extra-ordinary leadership profile and plans with a friend or trusted colleague. Remember to take some time just for yourself. Remember to ask how you can do some good for someone else. Who can benefit from what you have to give? How can you begin today to make the world a better place? These questions are important to your development. Good questions will lead you further along the path of the extra-ordinary leader.

Helpful hints . . .

We have come to believe that having a central focus for your thoughts and efforts is a vital key to long-lasting achievement that is satisfying. You may not yet be aware of what your focus will be, so if that's true for you then your focus should be on *exploring* and the *discovery* of your focus. The activities in this book provide you with the raw materials through which you can ponder and sort. This exploratory process will take a measure of courage on your part as you take risks to step outside your comfort zone. Taking calculated risks with careful consideration of the facts at hand will do wonders for building your leadership

'Find a need and fill it.'

Ruth Stafford Peale

skills. This is a creative process so remind yourself to be patient with the uncertainty. There will be times when you'll want to move quickly and decisively, but there will be other times when it will be better to wait and watch. If you listen carefully during the quiet times you just might hear the sound of your self growing, despite the noise of uncertainty.

Resources and further reading

Bennis, W. and Nanus, B. (1985) *Leaders: The strategies for taking charge*, New York: Harper and Row Publishers

Cook, J. (1997) *The Book of Positive Quotations*, Fairview Press, Minneapolis

Fleetham, M. (2006) *Multiple Intelligences in Practice*, NCE

Fleetham, M. (2007) *Multiple Intelligences Pocket Pal*, NCE

Gardner, H. (1983) *Frames of Mind: The Theory of Multiple Intelligences*, New York: Basic Books

Gardner, H. (1993*) Creating Minds: An Anatomy of Creativity Seen Through the Lives of Freud, Einstein, Picasso, Stravinsky, Eliot, Graham, and Gandhi*, New York: Basic Books

Gardner, H. (1995*) Leading Minds: An Anatomy of Leadership*, New York: Basic Books

Gardner, H. (1997*) Extraordinary Minds: Portraits of 4 Exceptional Individuals and an Examination of Our Own Extraordinariness*, New York: Basic Books

Gardner, H. (1999) *Intelligence Reframed: Multiple Intelligences for the 21st century*, New York: Basic Books

Goleman, D. (1995) *Emotional Intelligence*, New York: Bantam Books

Greenleaf, R. (1970) *Servant as Leader* (available at www.greenleaf.org)

Langer, E. (2005) *On Becoming an Artist: Reinventing Yourself Through Mindful Creativity*, Ballantine Books

National Commission on Excellence in Education (1983) *A Nation at Risk: The Imperative for Educational Reform* (www.ed.gov/pubs/NatAtRisk/index.html)

Shearer, C. B. (2000) *Common Miracles in Your School!* Kent, Ohio: Multiple Intelligences Research and Consulting, Inc

Shearer, C. B. (2000) *The MIDAS Handbook of Multiple Intelligences in the Classroom*, Kent, Ohio: Multiple Intelligences Research and Consulting, Inc

Shearer, C. B. (2006) *An Integrated Model of Multiple Intelligences: Integrating Triarchic, IQ, EQ and MI Theories* (available at www.miresearch.org/research.php)

Shearer, C. B. (2007) *The MIDAS Professional Manual: Revised*, Kent, Ohio: Multiple Intelligences Research and Consulting, Inc (available from the author via www.miresearch.org or email sbranton@kent.edu)

Sternberg, R. J. (1985) *Beyond IQ: The Triarchic Theory of Human Intelligence*, New

York: Cambridge University Press

Further Information

Branton's website: http://www.miresearch.com

Mike's website: http://www.thinkingclassroom.co.uk

This book's wikispace: http://extraordinary-teachers.wikispace.com/